SECOND EDITION

Words and **Actions:**

Teaching Languages Through the Lens of Social Justice

Cassandra Glynn
Concordia College, Moorhead

Pamela Wesely
University of Iowa

Beth Wassell
Rowan University

ACTFL AMERICAN COUNCIL ON THE
TEACHING OF FOREIGN LANGUAGES

*For our families, students, and fellow language teachers
and teacher educators. You inspire and motivate us.*

The American Council on the Teaching of Foreign Languages
1001 North Fairfax Street, Suite 200
Alexandria, VA 22314

Graphic Design by Paintbox Creative, LLC
Edited by Todd Larson

© 2014 by The American Council on the Teaching of Foreign Languages, Alexandria, VA
Second edition, 2018

ISBN: 978-1-942544-63-0

Table of Contents

Acknowledgments

We are thankful to a wide variety of people for their support of this project. First and foremost, the American Council on the Teaching of Foreign Languages (ACTFL) has been integral to our development as teachers and teacher educators, and we are very proud to be able to publish the second edition of this book under their name. We appreciate Chief Operating Officer Howie Berman, Director of Education Paul Sandrock, and Executive Director Marty Abbott for supporting this project, encouraging it, and providing us with feedback on it.

Many others also contributed to this second edition in very important ways. A number of our esteemed colleagues gave us crucial feedback that enabled us to expand and enhance the second edition, including Martha Bigelow, Jason Martel, Alyssa Warne, Alice Yang, and the Spring 2018 Obermann Fellows-in-Residence group at the University of Iowa. We also thank Stacey Margarita Johnson and L.J. Randolph for their leadership and vision for the Critical and Social Justice Approaches Special Interest Group (SIG), who have provided us a structure for the book, as well as colleagues to share resources and collaborate on key issues related to equity in our field.

We owe great thanks to the teachers who contributed their ideas, perspectives, questions and suggestions on teaching social justice in world language classrooms. Thank you to Caroline Brachet, Christen Campbell, Joan Clifford, Carmel deGuzman, Richard de Meij, Mary Devine, Gary DiBianca, Madji Fall, Katherine Farley, Christopher Gwin, Annam Hasan, Krishauna Hines-Gaither, Jennifer Hoban, Brandon Locke, Diane Neubauer, Catherine Ousselin, Stephanie Owen-Lyons, Luzbette Russo, Monica Stillman, Reuben Vyn, and Molly Wieland. We are proud to call them colleagues in the field of world language teaching.

We are especially grateful to our colleagues who shared their creative, original units, which can be found throughout the text and in the Appendix. Thank you to Sara Biondi, Becky Blankenship, Taliá González, Whitney Hellenbrand, Elissabeth Legendre, Leyla Masmaliyeva, Diane Neubauer, Fanny Roncal Ramirez, Lara Ravitch, Reed Riggs, Asma Ben Romdhane, Ngan-Ha Ta, and Alyssa Warne for your willingness to share your work with our teaching community. We are so inspired by their continual work in addressing issues of injustice and inequity in their world language classrooms.

We would like to thank Terry Osborn, a pioneer in social justice in world language education, for both supporting our work and for writing the Foreword to our second edition. We are humbled by his contribution.

We appreciate the generosity and collegiality of all of the individuals who gave feedback and directly contributed to this book. That said, all errors, both factual and conceptual, are solely the responsibility of the three authors.

We would also like to thank Concordia College, Rowan University, and the University of Iowa, our three employers, for supporting us in our scholarly endeavors. We have all built this work from the experiences and knowledge cultivated with language teaching organizations and institutions including the Center for Applied Research in Language Acquisition (CARLA) at the University of Minnesota and Concordia Language Villages. We extend our thanks to them as well, and to all of the primary, secondary and post-secondary schools that have supported our development as students and teachers over the years.

Finally, we would like to thank our families for their invaluable support in this project, and always.

Foreword

Language teaching is a *political* act. By *political,* I do not mean that language teaching, per se, is an activity of Republicans, Democrats or any other political party (though it certainly could be used to support a political agenda). I invoke the definition of *political* articulated by the Collins English Dictionary, "relating to the way power is achieved and used in a country or society."[1]

Put another way, it is helpful to understand that language teaching is not merely developing or facilitating proficiency in a language. Language teaching is an activity that, by way of examples, either explicitly or implicitly:

- makes claims about what a language is, and is not;

- makes claims about where a language is spoken, and where it is not spoken;

- makes claims about who sets rules as to what is "correct" and "incorrect" in terms of language use;

- makes claims about the status of language varieties within the "home culture" where the language is taught and learned;

- makes claims about the native language(s) of the students and the teacher; and

- produces or reproduces structures of power in a country or society.

Twenty years ago, these issues were poorly understood in the foreign language teaching profession. Even less understood was what teachers were to do, given these truths.

Today there is a different reality, thanks to the work of scholars such as Cassandra Glynn, Pamela Wesely, and Beth Wassell. This generation of world language education scholarship no longer accepts the implied assignment to treat language teaching as a journey through exotica of cultural trivia and linguistic norming. Instead, they understand that language and power are interdependent and inextricable. Therefore, it is impossible to be politically neutral as a world language teacher, because what becomes part of the explicit curriculum, the implicit curriculum, and the null curriculum in a classroom is based on the often contradictory societal struggles.

The challenge to change how we teach languages is complex. We must, in my view, hold at least three tensions in balance successfully. First, we must face the dynamic tension of prescribing how to teach while not defining social justice for others. If we seek to give word-for-word scripts of how to teach for social justice, we permit no opportunity for the local realities of language diversity (a process I referred to as microcontextualization).[2] Put another way, preparing teachers with a lens of social justice requires a pedagogy of humility.

Second, we must face balancing the demands of proficiency with the opportunities for a critical meta-awareness of language. Students should not be left with the dichotomy of either learning a language or learning about a language. Both proficiency and social justice are important. It is likely duplicitous to claim to promote social justice monolingually in a world language classroom. At the same time, treating language in any given society as apolitical is similarly ill-conceived.

Finally, language teachers must understand the balance between building understanding today and support for tomorrow. In the early twentieth century, the language teaching profession found itself in the throes of an internal

---

[1] Collins English Dictionary. (2018). Definition of 'political.' *Collins.* Retrieved June 24, 2018, from https://www.collinsdictionary.com/us/dictionary/english/political.

[2] Osborn, T. A. (2005). *Critical reflection and the foreign language classroom* (rev. ed.). Greenwich, CT: Information Age Publishing.

battle between German and Spanish based on which language was more politically palatable, even as both struggled to be considered as legitimate as the classics.[3] The change in world language education will not happen overnight, but as it becomes less exotic, it will also become less esoteric. Indeed, a relevant world language educational experience will enjoy much support for increased funding and study. An irrelevant language learning experience permits neither speaking about a second language nor speaking in one.

This newest edition of *Words and Actions: Teaching Languages Through the Lens of Social Justice* illuminates the trail of our journey forward in days of increasing political polarization. As I write this, there is a significant outcry in the United States concerning the separation of children from their parents at our border with Mexico. The President of the United States has just issued an executive order banning the practice. It is my sincere hope that all world language classes are discussing the complex issues surrounding the situation. I hope that somewhere a Christian student from a red state and a Muslim student from a blue state are finding common ground across the political spectrum in a dialogue about what is right and just. And, just maybe, that conversation began in their world language classroom after a critical moment. It is time, indeed, for our words to become actions.

Terry A. Osborn, Ph.D.
Sarasota, Florida

---

[3] Herman, D. M. (2002). "Our Patriotic Duty": Insights from professional history, 1890-1920. In T. A. Osborn (ed.), *The future of foreign language education in the United States,* 1-30. Westport, CT: Bergin & Garvey.

Preface

Seven years ago, the idea of writing a book for teachers about teaching for and about social justice was born at the American Council on the Teaching of Foreign Languages (ACTFL) convention in Denver. Just a few years later, in 2014, ACTFL published *Words and Actions,* through which we were honored to share our ideas and work with teachers. Since the publication of the first edition, we have been both inspired and energized by the social justice instruction happening in world language classrooms at varied levels and in diverse contexts. In our workshops and conversations with world language teachers, it became apparent that a new edition of *Words and Actions* was necessary to address the many new ideas and questions teachers had shared with us since the first edition.

Our motivation for this project has remained the same: social justice, critical pedagogy, and culturally sustaining teaching are central to our educational philosophies. Like us, both pre-service and in-service teachers strive to address social justice topics that occur regularly within the various spaces they occupy. Furthermore, we acknowledge how diverse many teachers' schools are, and social justice education affirms and empowers minoritized and marginalized students. We are also aware of the need to teach for social justice in monocultural classrooms and schools, a characteristic that still describes some of the world language classrooms in which teachers find themselves. Students from both multicultural and monocultural classrooms will emerge from their educational experiences into a complex, multicultural, multilingual world, and world language teachers are well positioned to prepare students to move between various spaces in an empathetic, open, responsive manner.

Over the last four years, our understanding of social justice in world language education has expanded, in large part due to our experiences with K-16 language teachers who are redefining what is possible in world language classrooms. We have continued to question mainstream teaching of language and culture, and our emphasis on social justice remains, in part, a way to expand the definition and scope of world language education. This will lead to further innovation in the field and to language learning experiences that are welcoming and meaningful for all students.

This new edition more clearly defines what social justice looks like in the classroom, to help readers better navigate the differences between a good cultural lesson, for example, and a social justice lesson. Both certainly have their place in the world language classroom, so teachers must be able to discern what social justice is and is not. Additionally, we have expanded Chapter 4 beyond adapting textbook-driven curricula to include other language learning contexts and approaches to language teaching, and we have included examples from diverse curricula. The opportunity to connect and collaborate with many teachers over the last four years has also enabled us to provide more examples from different languages, which we hope will give knowledgeable social justice-minded language teachers a voice. Finally, we have included a new chapter about critical moments in the classroom, which is integral to teaching for social justice. Since it can be hard to address certain comments and events in the classroom, we strived to provide explicit tools for teachers to do so.

We hope this new edition will make you feel inspired, encouraged, and supported by colleagues in the field who are doing this work alongside you. We also hope it will help you find a path forward to teaching for and about social justice in the world language classroom in a way meaningful and impactful for you and your students.

CHAPTER 1
Introduction

When students step into a world language classroom, they enter an environment the teacher has carefully crafted, where visuals, music, and the sound of the language fill their senses. You may remember being a student of world language yourself, and how entering the classroom transported you into new experiences and worlds, even in the space of a short class. In this chapter, we will explain why the environments world language teachers create in the classroom must address issues of social justice. We will begin with an overview and definition of social justice education and related terms, and then we will summarize our rationale for a systematic inclusion of social justice instruction in the world language classroom. Then we will connect central notions in social justice education with the standards and skills that frame contemporary world language education. Finally, we will conclude with a preview of the rest of the book.

A Glimpse into the Classroom

Margaret and Josie are two high-school French teachers who have been working on perfecting the scope and sequence for the Levels 1 through Advanced Placement (AP) courses they offer in their school. They selected a good textbook, and their students react well to it and tend to score well on standardized tests in French. However, these teachers have become increasingly aware of the world's inequities and injustices, both in the cultures they study and even among their students. They have also realized that their students are often unaware of these issues and draw on stereotypes or misconceptions instead of trying to question or understand these issues in depth.

Margaret and Josie want to incorporate some of these issues into their French curriculum but are having trouble figuring out where to start. They are worried that they lack training in social justice education and will make mistakes that will impede their progress. They are both concerned that time and resources are short, too. Margaret, who has taught the AP French class for a long time, loves the les-

sons that she has created over her years of teaching. She does not want to get rid of everything that she has already done, especially because her students achieve good results on the AP exam. Josie, who was born and raised in Madagascar, wants to discuss some of the social justice issues in African countries with her students, but she is worried about reinforcing their stereotypes or making them feel that social justice is someone else's problem on another continent.

To think through the vignette, please answer these questions:

1. Do you share any concerns with Margaret and Josie about social justice in your current or future world language classroom? What are those concerns?

2. What other concerns do you have about incorporating social justice education into your world language class?

What is Social Justice Education?

Before beginning our discussion of how to incorporate social justice education into the world language curriculum and classroom, we are going to begin with a broader view of what social justice education means. Scholars, activists, educators and others who work to support human rights, equity, and fairness have suggested many different definitions of social justice. Sonia Nieto defines **social justice** as "a philosophy, an approach, and actions that embody treating all people with fairness, respect, dignity, and generosity" (2010, p. 46). She suggests that **social justice education** includes the following four components:

1. It *challenges, confronts, and disrupts* misconceptions, untruths, and stereotypes that lead to structural inequality and discrimination based on social and human differences.

2. It provides *all* students with the *resources* necessary to learn to their full potential, including both material and emotional resources.

3. It draws on the *talents and strengths* students bring to their education.

4. It creates a learning environment that promotes *critical thinking* and agency for social change.

According to this conceptualization, all teachers and students are beneficiaries of social justice education. That is, social justice education is not targeted to benefit a certain group or set of groups; it benefits all.

Hackman's Five Components of Social Justice Education

To identify whether a specific classroom approach or activity could constitute social justice education, we find the model below provided by Hackman (2005) to be particularly useful (Fig. 1.1).

Without all of these five components, a lesson, activity or curriculum cannot be deemed a form of social justice education. **As we look at these components, consider one or more examples from your own educational experience (as a teacher, colleague, or student) that you consider to constitute social justice education. Do they include all five components?**

Content Mastery and Factual Information. This is the first step. It includes factual information, its historical context, and a macro-to-micro analysis of the content. Without content mastery and factual information, students lack the foundation upon which to build and learn.

Tools for Critical Analysis. However, a focus on content is not sufficient to be considered social justice education. Hackman (2005) argues that tools for critical analysis are necessary because information alone does not necessarily lead to deep understanding, nor does it inherently provide students with agency for action. Additionally, Hackman suggests that it is important to note that all content should be viewed through a critical lens and open for debate. Depending on the context and manner in which the content is delivered, it could lead to further marginalization if opportunities for critical analysis are not present.

Tools for Social Action and Change. These engender students' agency and empower them to see that they have the potential to work toward change, whether as allies or as members of marginalized communities.

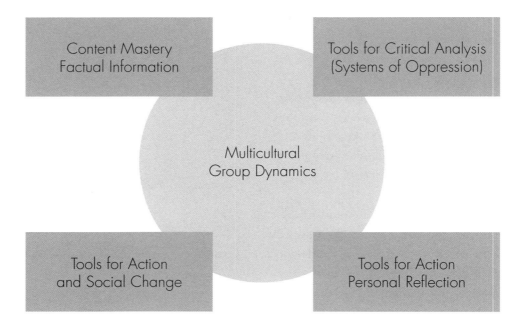

Figure 1.1. Five components of social justice education (Hackman, 2005)

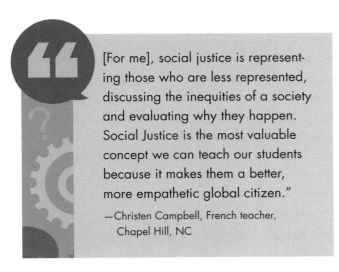

> "[For me], social justice is representing those who are less represented, discussing the inequities of a society and evaluating why they happen. Social Justice is the most valuable concept we can teach our students because it makes them a better, more empathetic global citizen."
>
> —Christen Campbell, French teacher, Chapel Hill, NC

Tools for Personal Reflection. These provide a powerful space for teachers and students to reflect on their own experiences, perceptions, and roles (Hackman, 2005). (Examples of moving from the exploration of content to action can be found throughout the book, and reflection will be discussed further in Chapter 7.)

Multicultural Group Dynamics. Finally, a teacher's awareness of multicultural group dynamics determines how the other components may be addressed in the classroom. The teacher must not only understand students' identities but also create a student-centered, respectful environment in which critical discussion can take place and students can thrive (Hackman, 2005). (Strategies for building community and developing an awareness of one's identity, along with those of one's students will be examined in Chapter 2.)

Now think back on the example(s) that you thought of that you feel illustrate teaching for social justice. Were all five of these components present? What changes could have been made to address these components more thoroughly?

Teaching Tolerance's Social Justice Standards

To connect social justice education more specifically with what is done in the classroom, let us look at Teaching Tolerance's *Social Justice Standards* (2016), which outline four domains: Identity, Diversity, Justice, and Action. Within these domains, the authors provide twenty Anchor Standards, five per domain (Fig. 1.2).

These standards provide "a common language and organizational structure" (Teaching Tolerance, 2016, p. 2). They are not a curriculum, but rather a tool for curriculum development. As we proceed through this chapter and the rest of the book, we will use these standards alongside the *World-Readiness Standards for Learning Languages* (The National Standards Collaborative Board, 2015), the standards commonly used in the United States for world language education.

Related Concepts and Terminology

Several key concepts are central to teaching for and about social justice in the world languages classroom: **equality, equity, privilege, marginalization, oppression, dehumanization, culturally relevant pedagogy,** and **culturally sustaining pedagogy.** These concepts are complex and have been defined in many ways throughout the literature, but they represent an important foundation as we think about how to weave social justice into the classroom. As Rahima Wade articulated, "If we are to teach for and about social justice, understanding what it looks, sounds, and feels like is critical" (Wade, 2007, p. 4). To create this foundation, we provide our working definitions of these terms here:

Equality in education can be defined as providing equal access to funding, learning opportunities, resources, assistance, etc., so that all students have the same chances to succeed and no student is denied something that the teacher or school has provided to the rest of the students. On the other hand, the notion of **equity** suggests that teachers must also recognize the differences among their students and differentiate accordingly. For example, some students need additional resources, attention, or encouragement to be successful, and teachers who seek equity in the classroom would access resources or differentiate instruction based on students' individual needs.

Individuals in any context, such as a classroom, have the potential to bring more or less **privilege,** defined as the advantages, favors, and benefits to which they have access based on their gender, race, class, sexual orientation, native language, or another element of their identity. In her seminal essay, Peggy McIntosh (1989) describes privilege as "an invisible package of unearned assets" (p. 9). Privilege is often available to members of dominant groups in a society at the expense of members of nondominant or **marginalized** groups. Marginalization relegates a group of people to the "margins" of society or confines them to an inferior social position. It is often seen as a form of **oppression,** the unjust exertion of power over a group, and **dehumanization,** the taking away of one's humanity (Freire, 1993). Teaching for and about social justice has the power to make each of these concepts explicit, understandable, and relevant for students, an important first step toward action.

Moreover, teaching for social justice can be closely related to a number of similar topics, not all of which will be emphasized in this book. Perhaps the foremost of these concepts is **multicultural education,** which focuses on understanding the history, contributions, struggles and perspectives of diverse groups of people. For Banks and McGee Banks (2012) multicultural education has multiple dimensions: it is a concept that articulates all students' right to learn, a movement for educational reform, and a process, since "educational equity, like liberty and justice, is an ideal toward which all humans work, but never fully attain" (p. 4).

Identity Domain

I-1. Students will develop positive social identities based on their membership in multiple groups in society.

I-2. Students will develop language and historical and cultural knowledge that affirm and accurately describe their membership in multiple identity groups.

I-3. Students will recognize that people's multiple identities interact and create unique and complex individuals.

I-4. Students will express pride, confidence and healthy self-esteem without denying the value and dignity of other people.

I-5. Students will recognize traits of the dominant culture, their home culture and other cultures and understand how they negotiate their own identity in multiple spaces.

Justice Domain

J-11. Students will recognize stereotypes and relate to people as individuals rather than representatives of groups.

J-12. Students will recognize unfairness on the individual level (e.g., biased speech) and injustice at the institutional or systemic level (e.g., discrimination).

J-13. Students will analyze the harmful impact of bias and injustice on the world, historically and today.

J-14. Students will recognize that power and privilege influence relationships on interpersonal, intergroup and institutional levels and consider how they have been affected by those dynamics.

J-15. Students will identify figures, groups, events and a variety of strategies and philosophies relevant to the history of social justice around the world.

Diversity Domain

D-6. Students will express comfort with people who are both similar to and different from them and engage respectfully with all people.

D-7. Students will develop language and knowledge to accurately and respectfully describe how people (including themselves) are both similar to and different from each other and others in their identity groups.

D-8. Students will respectfully express curiosity about the history and lived experiences of others and will exchange ideas and beliefs in an open-minded way.

D-9. Students will respond to diversity by building empathy, respect, understanding and connection.

D-10. Students will examine diversity in social, cultural, political and historical contexts rather than in superficial or oversimplified ways.

Action Domain

A-16. Students will express empathy when people are excluded or mistreated because of their identities and concern when they themselves experience bias.

A-17. Students will recognize their own responsibility to stand up to exclusion, prejudice and injustice.

A-18. Students will speak up with courage and respect when they or someone else has been hurt or wronged by bias.

A-19. Students will make principled decisions about when and how to take a stand against bias and injustice in their everyday lives and will do so despite negative peer or group pressure.

A-20. Students will plan and carry out collective action against bias and injustice in the world and will evaluate what strategies are most effective.

Figure 1.2. Teaching Tolerance's Social Justice Standards (2016)

Asset pedagogies like **culturally relevant pedagogy** and **culturally sustaining pedagogy** are approaches to teaching that recognize and build on students' cultures as an important source for their education (Ladson-Billings, 1995; Nieto, 2010; Paris & Alim, 2017). Paris and Alim (2017) explain that "culturally sustaining pedagogy seeks to perpetuate and foster—to sustain linguistic, literate and cultural pluralism for positive social transformation," a purpose that naturally aligns with the work we do in world languages classrooms (p. 1). Culturally sustaining pedagogy and other asset pedagogies are central elements of social justice education, and we will discuss it as a part of our first steps to implementing social justice education in the classroom in Chapter 2.

Why Incorporate Social Justice into World Language Education?

Stakeholders including students, teachers, families, school administrators, and anyone else with a "stake" in world language education often see world language classes as primarily a way for students to secure better jobs and meet workplace demands. These pragmatic, instrumental purposes for world language education are very important, and we do not argue that they should be deemphasized. Nonetheless, world language educators have the opportunity to move beyond imparting language skills as the sole focus of their instruction.

Stakeholders have begun to see the importance of learning a language as a way to interact respectfully and responsively with members of the target communities. These ideas are identified as **global competence,** which ACTFL defines as including "the ability to communicate with respect and cultural understanding in more than one language" (ACTFL, 2014), and **intercultural communicative competence,** wherein an individual can see relationships among different cultures and mediate among them (Byram, 2000). Frameworks in world language education have echoed the need for these competences, like the *21st Century Skills Map for World Language Education* (ACTFL & P21, 2011) and the *NCSSFL-ACTFL Intercultural Communication Can-Do Statements* (2017). These competences also connect closely with teaching for social justice in the world language classroom.

"World language teachers and global studies teachers should be leaders in our school communities in the areas of social justice and global citizenship. We should be opening our students' eyes to the world, definite ways of living, thinking, as well as the injustices. We should be teaching our students to be globally competent and compassionate."

—Jennifer Hoban, French teacher, Lexington, KY

Furthermore, we stand with our colleagues in the fields of critical pedagogy and multicultural education in our belief that "All pedagogical efforts are infiltrated with value judgments and cross hatched by vectors of power serving particular interests in the name of certain regimes of truth" (Sleeter & McLaren, 1995, p. 18). That is, teachers teach more than the content area; they teach students how to think, whom to trust, what to believe, what to value, and more. Education is not neutral; it is inherently political.

In this book, we integrate these concepts to present a systematic, sequenced, easy-to-implement approach that both pre-service and in-service teachers can use in their world language classrooms. But why? Our reasons for advocating for this approach align with the four domains and the Anchor Standards of Teaching Tolerance's *Social Justice Standards* (2016) (Fig. 1.2).

Identity Domain

The Identity Domain and its Anchor Standards address the importance of student understanding of the nature of their identities and those of others. In the world language classroom, we can invite students to look closely at cultures and customs of other nations. We can extend this beyond the visible to the invisible, from holidays to accessing resources, from clothing to identity markers. In identifying these parts of other cultures, we invite students to compare and examine their own cultures and identities. As students learn all of the different ways others can be Mexican, Chinese, French, or German, for example, they also reflect on what it means to be from the United States (Anchor Standard I-2, I-3). Scholars have often warned against seeing students as "passive recipients of an immutable culture," and world language teachers can draw their students' attention to the parts of their own culture in equal measure with other cultures (González, 2005, p. 36). This echoes Anchor Standard I-5, which calls for students to "recognize traits of the dominant culture, their home culture and other cultures and understand how they negotiate their own identity in multiple spaces." By engaging students of all abilities and backgrounds in the conversation, we are more likely to have a positive effect on practices in the future (Swalwell, 2013).

Diversity Domain

The Diversity Domain and its Anchor Standards focus on how students develop their awareness of ways people can be similar and different. Looking at differences between the target cultures and the students' languages and cultures is central to much of the work done in the world language classroom. World language teachers can thus help students to develop the language and knowledge to describe similarities and differences with respectful curiosity (Anchor Standards D-7). If the ability to care authentically about others and to demonstrate empathy, respect, understanding, and connection (Anchor Standard D-9) is instilled in students within the world language classroom environment, they will develop a deeper understanding of both their own culture and the target culture. They will also develop the competence to communicate with those different from themselves, exchanging ideas and beliefs in an open-minded way (Anchor Standard D-8). Apple (2013) reminds us that, "care, love and solidarity – or the absence of them – are among the constitutive building blocks of one's identity" (p. 20).

Justice Domain

The Justice Domain focuses on helping students to look at bias and injustice, as well as at power and privilege, at a number of levels, from individual to systemic. World language teachers have a unique opportunity to help students question their stereotypes and myths about people living

in other cultures (Anchor Standard J-11). Identifying differences can be an important first step to recognizing unfairness, bias, and injustice (Anchor Standard J-12); developing our curricula further in this respect is a development, but not a new direction. In our examinations of the histories and societies of the cultures we study, we can also look at bias and injustice in the world (Anchor Standard J-13), as well as figures, groups, and events that played a role in those societies (Anchor Standard J-14). Helping students to think critically about power dynamics and social change in other cultures can help them to see things they might not see in their own culture.

Action Domain

Action is vital to teaching for social justice. We cannot teach our students about social justice simply as a concept, devoid of any real-world applications or relevance. With the rise of service learning and project-based learning in world language classrooms, many world language teachers have already laid important groundwork for working for action in their classrooms. This action can be done via projects in which students advocate for members of the target community in their local context or for members of the target culture in other countries or locations (Anchor Standard A-18, A-20). Students can use their language skills to translate, express empathy, and stand up to exclusion, prejudice, and injustice (Anchor Standards A-16, A-17). In the authors' experience, taking action can be a challenging component of teaching for social justice for many world language teachers, but it is vital to the endeavor.

The *World-Readiness Standards* and Social Justice Education

Now that we have made some initial, general connections between social justice education and world language education, we will take the opposite perspective, and begin with the major standards in world language education, explaining more specifically how they can connect to social justice education. Hopefully, you are already familiar with the *World-Readiness Standards for Learning Languages* (The National Standards Collaborative Board, 2015), so this section will focus on helping you to see these standards in a new light.

The *World-Readiness Standards for Learning Languages* are the most recent incarnation of the National Standards, which were first published in 1996 by the American Council on the Teaching of Foreign Languages (ACTFL) (The National Standards Collaborative Board, 2015). We believe that starting with the World-Readiness Standards is beneficial for all world language teachers; research has shown that as many as 89% of current world language teachers are familiar with the Standards (Phillips & Abbott, 2011). Although some states have state-level world language standards, they are commonly adapted from the World-Readiness Standards. Sometimes called the "5 Cs," these Standards are organized under the five categories of *Communication, Cultures, Connections, Comparisons,* and *Communities* (Fig. 1.3). We expect that, if you are in a world language teacher education program in the United States, you are already somewhat familiar with these Standards. So we will focus on connecting them with the prospect of addressing social justice issues in the classroom.

Communication

Communicate effectively in more than one language in order to function in a variety of situations and for multiple purposes

- Interpersonal Communication: Learners interact and negotiate meaning in spoken, signed, or written conversations to share information, reactions, feelings, and opinions.

- Interpretive Communication: Learners understand, interpret, and analyze what is heard, read, or viewed on a variety of topics.

- Presentational Communication: Learners present information, concepts, and ideas to inform, explain, persuade, and narrate on a variety of topics using appropriate media and adapting to various audiences of listeners, readers, or viewers.

Cultures

Interact with cultural competence and understanding

- Relating Cultural Practices to Perspectives: Learners use the language to investigate, explain, and reflect on the relationship between the practices and perspectives of the cultures studied.

- Relating Cultural Products to Perspectives: Learners use the language to investigate, explain, and reflect on the relationship between the products and perspectives of the cultures studied.

Connections

Connect with other disciplines and acquire information and diverse perspectives in order to use the language to function in academic and career-related situations

- Making Connections: Learners build, reinforce, and expand their knowledge of other disciplines while using the language to develop critical thinking and to solve problems creatively.

- Acquiring Information and Diverse Perspectives: Learners access and evaluate information and diverse perspectives that are available through the language and its cultures.

Comparisons

Develop insight into the nature of language and culture in order to interact with cultural competence

- Language Comparisons: Learners use the language to investigate, explain, and reflect on the nature of language through comparisons of the language studied and their own.

- Cultural Comparisons: Learners use the language to investigate, explain, and reflect on the concept of culture through comparisons of the cultures studied and their own.

Communities

Communicate and interact with cultural competence in order to participate in multilingual communities at home and around the world

- School and Global Communities: Learners use the language both within and beyond the classroom to interact and collaborate in their community and the globalized world.

- Lifelong Learning: Learners set goals and reflect on their progress in using languages for enjoyment, enrichment, and advancement.

Figure 1.3. World-Readiness Standards for Learning Languages (The National Standards Collaborative Board, 2015)

These Standards and their components clearly lend themselves to addressing social justice issues. The *Communication* Standard suggests that students do more than read, write, speak, and listen in the target language. They must analyze, negotiate meaning, persuade, and adapt to audiences. Their interaction with the language is a personal process, one that makes them find appropriate resources, whether those are material resources or their talents and strengths in the classroom. The *Cultures* Standard, which relates the products and practices of a culture to the perspectives of its individuals, will be a guiding framework for much of how we will identify social justice issues, as you will read later in this chapter. Both components of the *Connections* Standard suggest social justice connections, since the Standard addresses both critical thinking and the access to diverse perspectives. *Comparisons,* as mentioned above, are necessary for identifying the social and human differences identified as one of the starting points for social justice education (Nieto, 2010). By comparing the cultures studied with their own, our students learn how differences among people can present both challenges and insights. Finally, *Communities,* with its focus on collaborating and interacting with others in the globalized world, encourages students to familiarize themselves with issues in a variety of contexts. It also offers a pathway to action.

Throughout this book we will refer back to these Standards. As you begin to craft and adapt your own lessons, we will ask you to identify the Standards that you plan to meet in those lessons.

Social Justice Issues and Social Justice Activities in this Book

Social justice education can be integrated into all levels of world language education. One quick example from the world language classroom is the vocabulary commonly taught about professions. When we use a lens of social justice to teach these lessons, which professions are taught? Which are not taught? What do the visual representations used in the textbook, on posters, on worksheets, or on visual flash cards say about who typically works in each profession? Do they reveal gender, racial, or ethnic stereotypes? Additionally, are the words provided for the professions the same across *all* cultures that use that language?

If not, which words are privileged? These issues persist regardless of which language teaching methods are used in the classroom. For instance, in a world language classroom where the curriculum is structured around storytelling, a story might focus on a transaction in a store. How do the customer and the seller behave? What does the customer seek, and how is that shown to have value? And even more globally, why do we focus on professions and exchanges of money in the first levels of language learning so ubiquitously? Each of these questions can help us to think more deeply about the content we teach in world languages and the ways we commonly teach it.

In this section, we will suggest some types of social justice issues and activities that can provide a starting point for considering how you might integrate social justice education into your own world language curriculum.

Categories of Social Justice Issues

In this book, we map our categories of social justice issues on the components of culture, as established in the World-Readiness Standard addressing Culture (The National Standards Collaborative Board, 2015). These include: **products,** both tangible and intangible; behavioral **practices;** and philosophical **perspectives.** More precisely, products include things people have: books, tools, foods, laws, music, games, etc. Practices focus on what people do, or patterns of social interactions. Perspectives include meanings, attitudes, values, and ideas.

Although what we often colloquially call the "three Ps" are stand-alone categories, the World-Readiness Standards outline the relationship among them (Fig. 1.2). Therefore, we also recommend that teachers think of these three different categories of social justice issues as interrelated and connected, with both the products and the practices primarily important in how they relate to the perspectives.

In this book, we focus on the following types of social justice issues:

1. **Products:** Social justice issues that focus on access to and relationships with tangible and intangible resources. Examples might include:

- How access to clean water affects developing countries and communities

- The ways immigration laws shape decisions made by individuals

- Educational systems and language policy

2. **Practices:** Social justice issues that arise from how people interact. Examples might include:

- Activist movements and how they achieve their goals

- Language usage and its implications in specific contexts (schools, jobs, etc.)

- Ways communities express themselves in the face of oppression

3. **Perspectives:** Social justice issues stemming from attitudes and values. Examples might include:

- How beliefs about the humanity of individual groups affect their access to employment

- The evolution of beliefs about homosexuality and marriage laws in the target cultures

- The ways politicians and political writers express beliefs through speeches

Many places can give rise to social justice issues we can address. See Appendix A for some selected themes, activity ideas, and online resources for inspiration. Another source for identifying social justice issues is the United Nations' *Sustainable Development Goals* (2012).

Categories of Social Justice Activities

There are many ways to think about the different types of social justice activities in the world language classroom. By **social justice activities,** we mean, very broadly, *planned* classroom-based learning events that address social justice issues. We contrast these activities with, for instance, the unplanned moments that arise during a class. We believe that those moments, too, are important aspects of social justice learning but not the focus of these categories.

Some teachers in the world language community have expressed concern about their ability to teach social justice understandings effectively at different proficiency levels, particularly the novice level. We have sought to address these issues, and we provide a very general way of thinking of social justice activities. We believe that all of these categories of activities can be adapted to different proficiency levels, tasks, lessons, or unit durations, and to different ages of students. Several parts of this book offer ample examples of these activities, and each example is labeled clearly with our suggested category of activity.

Finally, we are not attempting to argue that social justice can be addressed only through an activity that fits neatly in one of these categories. These categories merely provide a structure that can give us one among many ways of organizing our thoughts about social justice activities. We encourage all world language teachers to be creative and to adapt or blend these categories according to their own interests, talents, and experiences.

From most teacher-centered to most student-centered, our categories are:

1. **Problem-posing activities.** These activities, as suggested by Reagan and Osborn (2002), focus on discussion, critical inquiry, and interactive participation. The problems can be posed by students about cultural artifacts in their own culture or other cultures, and they can lead to reflection and examination of accepted truths by simply asking: "Why?"

2. **Text analysis activities.** Here, we use the broadest definition of the word text, which can mean not just the written word, but also the spoken word, audio and videotape, media elements, and even images with no written materials (Kramsch, 1993). These activities encompass some of the tasks often associated with media literacy, text analysis, and visual analysis.

3. **Rights and policy investigations.** This type of activity explores how groups and individuals might be affected by externally imposed rules and regulations, often in the form of policy and laws. These activities can also

focus on activism and voices that speak up against policies. They can be teacher-directed (i.e., through a teacher-provided news article), or student-directed (i.e., through a project focusing on a conflict or a political movement).

4. **Individual experience investigations.** Given the increased access to the Internet in all educational environments, many students are more able to communicate with different individuals around the world. By looking into individual experiences through face-to-face interviews, simulation activities, questioning via email or social media, or participating in an online community or network, students can see individual perspectives in new ways.

5. **Reflection activities.** Journaling, participating in multicultural awareness tasks, taking part in a simulation, consciously comparing themselves to others, and other similar activities can also prompt students to see how social justice issues may affect their daily lives.

What Is, and Is Not Teaching for Social Justice?

Many of the aforementioned activities and topics are common in all world language classrooms, even ones in which teaching for social justice is not prioritized. It is possible to teach excellent units and topics about the target culture(s) without addressing social justice. To provide a clear way to assess these examples, we will return to Hackman's (2005) five components of teaching for social justice: content mastery and factual information, tools for action, tools for personal reflection, tools for critical analysis, and multicultural group dynamics. As multicultural group dynamics are a feature of the classroom and not one specific activity, we will assume that these are present in all of the examples below.

As a first example, consider an educator who has his/her learners paint a mural in a community center including inspirational words in the target language, then doing a presentation for the school on their work. Although this might reflect content mastery, tools for action, and tools for personal reflection, it does not address tools for critical analysis. Without this critical component, the project does not teach for social justice. The educator could have

learners investigate the role of public art in expressing dissent and support in a target culture, select an art style that speaks to their own lives or experiences, and then use elements from that in the mural. That critical perspective would transform the project into one that directly addresses social justice.

A second example illustrates the difference between teaching for social justice with college-age students and with elementary students. A project might ask college students to compare and contrast how people typically dress and why they dress that way in two target cultures. Again, content mastery and factual knowledge are a part of this lesson, and we could also state that tools for personal reflection are a part of it as well. However, tools for action and social change and tools for critical analysis are not present. Comparing clothing is a cognitively simple activity that would not necessarily lead to appropriately complex critical analysis in college students. However, were this same project implemented with elementary students, they might develop critical analysis that are more developmentally appropriate for them. Furthermore, if the project includes planning for a clothing drive for members of the target culture who have faced a natural disaster, that would add tools for action and social change.

A third example involves a presentation in a high school class by a native speaker of the language to talk about growing up and attending school in the target culture. This may include content mastery, factual information, and tools for reflection, but it does not address tools for action and social change or for critical analysis. However, were that same guest speaker invited to comment on their experience living or being an actor in a specific historical moment, the teacher could then invite students to read articles about others' experiences related to that moment. The students could then critically examine the variety of experiences and perspectives within that one event or movement. Finally, to add in the tools for action and social change, the students could come up with a reflection on how they would have reacted in that same situation.

In these three examples, the components of content mastery and factual information, as well as personal reflection, are often addressed in world language projects and lessons. However, layering tools for critical analysis and tools for social change is crucial in truly formulating learning opportunities that lead to teaching for social justice in the world language classroom.

A Note on Backward Design, Differentiation, and Writing Curriculum

This book has another underlying framework that focuses on the mechanics and philosophy of curriculum design, rather than on course content. There are several approaches teachers use to create curriculum units for their world language classrooms. The steps we have provided are based on ideas from the **backward design** approach (Wiggins & McTighe, 2006) and concepts emphasized in *Teacher's Handbook: Contextualized Language Instruction* (Shrum & Glisan, 2010; see also Osborn, 2006; Reagan & Osborn, 2002) and *The Keys to Planning for Learning: Effective Curriculum, Unit, and Lesson Design* (Clementi & Terrill, 2017). We encourage you to consult these texts for additional ideas and support as you plan.

Based on Wiggins and McTighe's *Understanding by Design* (2006), we adhere to three basic stages for the unit planning in this book (see Figure 1.4).

Stage 1: Identify desired results. At this stage, we will encourage you to work from the various standards and skills we have outlined above, identifying the key objectives for your lesson.

Stage 2: Determine acceptable evidence. At this stage, we will ask you to consider how you will assess what the students have learned.

Stage 3: Plan learning experiences and instruction. At this stage, we will finally guide you through planning the activities you will direct or facilitate with your students.

We do not intend for this text to be an introduction to backward design; for such an introduction, we recommend the titles and authors listed earlier in this section. Rather, we use this approach to curriculum design as a point of departure in this book. As you will read in chapter three, we have both simplified and elaborated on the notion of backward design to help you create your own original unit plan. More information and additional steps and guidelines will be provided throughout the book.

Overview of this Book

The Chapters

In Chapter Two, we will explore ways for you to prepare yourself and your students for social justice education in the world language classroom. First, we will discuss how you, as the teacher, can explore your own frame of reference and how social justice education can reflect your own background and experiences. Then, we will encourage you to examine how you can guide students along in a similar exploration. We will conclude with a set of ideas for building learning communities in your classroom that bridge differences and lay a foundation for social justice education.

In Chapter Three, we will help you develop ideas for units that incorporate social justice. We will walk you through a process rooted in the backwards design approach (Wiggins & McTighe, 2006). You will begin by identifying the major understandings related to social justice that you believe would best be addressed in your world language classroom. Then you will devise a summative assessment. Finally, you will choose materials, topics, language structures, and communicative functions that will help your students to succeed on those assessments.

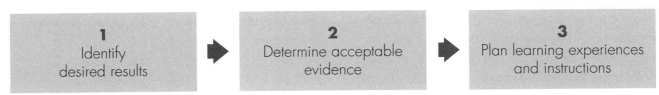

Figure 1.4. Stages of Backward Design (Wiggins & McTighe, 2006)

In Chapter Four, we will focus adapting your current curriculum to integrate social justice topics, and we will address multiple approaches to language teaching and types of curricula. We will provide detailed steps for adapting your existing units and lessons. We will guide you through ways to select parts of your curriculum that are easily expanded or connected with social justice issues. You will then be advised in how to develop and connect those parts with communicative approaches to social justice instruction.

In Chapter Five, we will turn the focus to lesson planning. You will connect the ideas that you developed in Chapters Three and Four, relating unit planning to lesson planning. Then, we will give you steps to an effective, social justice-focused lesson plan, helping you move from the general to the specific. This chapter offers suggestions for sequencing lessons, selecting appropriate activities, and integrating formative assessments.

Chapter Six is about handling critical moments in the classroom. We begin by describing critical moments that may arise in the language classroom, either unexpected or anticipated. We detail steps you can take to address the critical moment and maintain a classroom climate so students can maintain relationships with you and each other and can explore social justice issues. This chapter will also provide some ideas about how to build curriculum around critical moments and possible responses to several examples of critical moments.

Chapter Seven will focus on how to make room for reflection and self-assessment for everyone in your classroom, so as to maximize some of the learning that can go on during social justice instruction. First, we will provide a series of examples of how you can encourage students to reflect and self-assess, including self-assessment questionnaires, peer assessment, portfolios, and journaling, and then how you can incorporate reflection in your teaching, including before, during, and after social justice lessons. We will also connect your self-assessment with such teacher assessment frameworks as edTPA (Teacher Performance Assessment) and the Teacher Effectiveness for Language Learning (TELL) Project.

Chapter Eight will offer our perspectives on lingering questions you may have about social justice education. We will offer more specific suggestions about how to adapt your social justice instructions to different contexts, different student needs and abilities, and different philosophies. We will provide points to make when advocating for social justice education in your classroom or explaining it to your students and colleagues. Finally, we will offer some thoughts about how we hope the field will move forward.

The end of the book includes a number of detailed appendices, which will be referenced directly throughout the book. They include templates, lists of ideas and references, and general resources you can use to scaffold and develop your social justice instruction. We encourage you to use them liberally along with Chapters 1–8.

The Extra Features
Throughout the book, a few features will guide you through the chapters and help you reflect on your work. We will begin most chapters with invented teacher vignettes that illustrate some of the issues addressed in the chapter, followed by questions based on those vignettes to direct you through your initial thoughts on the topic. All of the vignettes are fictional, but based on a composite of real individuals and situations we have encountered in our work in pre-service and in-service teacher development. Since each of us works in different contexts, sometimes the most illustrative vignettes combine stories from multiple settings. We will also reference the experiences of individual teachers throughout the text; these examples are also composites assigned with invented names.

In addition, we include quotes from *real* teachers who incorporate social justice understandings into their classrooms in the book. We are very happy to include these voices; to collect them, we asked world language teachers of different backgrounds and experiences with teaching for social justice to share their perspectives. You will know which ones these are, because we give a first and last name and location.

Additionally, during the explanations and examples in each chapter, you will notice a special "Your Turn" icon after some sections:

This icon will invite you to put your own ideas into action, often to complete specific tasks related to developing curricular ideas or activities related to the content of that area of the book. We will provide blank templates for this work in most cases.

Finally, at the end of each chapter, there will be a set of discussion questions, designed to help you actively engage with the chapter content and expand your thinking in new directions followed by a list of references and additional readings that can provide more information on the chapter topic.

A Call to Action

In this chapter we have laid the foundation for thinking about teaching for and about social justice in world language classrooms. We hope you have gained a clearer understanding about what social justice is, as well as its potential for supporting students in thinking critically about rights, privileges, and justice in target cultures and beyond. However, teaching students about social justice is only one part of the puzzle. When students see us *model* compassion, empathy, advocacy, activism, and service, they will gain a more powerful understanding of its importance. Show your students how you speak up for those without a voice or how you take action toward an important issue that affects a target language community. Show them that social justice involves all of us working together toward change. Remember that "[s]ignificant global change will require the commitment of millions . . . there is room for all to take part" (Wade, 2007, p. 3).

Furthermore, social justice is not something that should wait until students have reached a certain proficiency level, are older, or are "ready" (Ennser-Kananen, 2016, p. 561). Now is the time to enact change in your classroom and in your students' lives and to empower them to be agents of change.

Discussion Questions

1. Look at Sonia Nieto's definition of social justice education (2010), then at Hackman's (2005) five components, then at Teaching Tolerance's Social Justice Standards (2016). What areas are emphasized in each one? Are there discrepancies among them? How would you use the three different ways of conceptualizing social justice education in your own work?

2. Which of the *World-Readiness Standards* (Fig. 1.3) do you think are most relevant to address in lessons that also address social justice issues? Which ones do you think would be the most challenging to combine with a focus on social justice? Choose a standard and imagine how it could be addressed in a lesson that also addresses social justice issues.

3. When is a vocabulary list more than a vocabulary list? Think about vocabulary you teach to your students (the example given in the text is professions). How does that list teach students more than just words? Does it impart any values? Does it situate you or your student in a particular social class? How could the choices one makes about vocabulary contribute to or reinforce stereotypes, values, or assumptions related to social class, race, gender, etc.?

4. Have you had any experiences in classrooms in which social justice education has occurred? Do not limit yourself to world language classrooms. Have you seen social justice education in action as a student, an observer, or a teacher? Reflect on how your experience, or lack thereof, might affect your experiences in creating lessons that address social justice.

REFERENCES

American Council on the Teaching of Foreign Languages. (2014). *Reaching global competence.* Retrieved from http://www.actfl.org/sites/default/files/GlobalCompetencePositionStatement0814.pdf

Apple, M. (2013). *Can education change society?* New York, NY: Routledge.

Banks, J. A., & McGee Banks, C. A. (2012). *Multicultural education: Issues and perspectives* (8th ed.). Hoboken, NJ: Wiley.

Byram, M. (2000). Assessing intercultural competence in language teaching. *Sprogforum*, 18(6), 8-13.

Chiariello, E., Edwards, J. O., Owen, N., Ronk, T., & Wicht, S. (2016). *Social justice standards: The teaching tolerance anti-bias framework.* Montgomery, AL: Teaching Tolerance, a Project of the Southern Poverty Law Center. Retrieved from https://www.tolerance.org/sites/default/files/2017-06/TT_Social_Justice_Standards_0.pdf

Ennser–Kananen, J. (2016). A pedagogy of pain: New directions for world language education. *The Modern Language Journal,* 100(2), 556-564.

Freire, P. (1993). *Pedagogy of the oppressed.* New York, NY: Continuum International Publishing Group.

Gay, G. (2010). *Culturally responsive teaching: Theory, research, and practice.* New York, NY: Teachers College Press.

González, N. (2005). Beyond culture: The hybridity of funds of knowledge. In N. González, L. Moll, & C. Amanti (Eds.), *Funds of knowledge: Theorizing practices in households, communities, and classrooms* (pp. 29-46). Mahwah, NJ: Lawrence Erlbaum.

Kramsch, C. (1993). *Context and culture in language teaching.* New York, NY: Oxford University Press.

Ladson-Billings, G. (1995). Toward a theory of culturally relevant pedagogy. *American Educational Research Journal,* 32(3), 465–491.

McIntosh, P. (1989). White privilege: Unpacking the invisible knapsack. *Peace and Freedom* (July/August 1989), 9-10. Retrieved from https://psychology.umbc.edu/files/2016/10/White-Privilege_McIntosh-1989.pdf

National Standards Collaborative Board. (2015). *World-Readiness Standards for Learning Languages.* 4th ed. Alexandria, VA: Author.

National Council of State Supervisors for Languages-American Council on the Teaching of Foreign Language (NCSSFL-ACTFL). (2017). *NCSSFL-ACTFL Can-Do Statements.* Alexandria, VA: American Council on the Teaching of Foreign Languages. Retrieved from https://www.actfl.org/publications/guidelines-and-manuals/ncssfl-actfl-can-do-statements

Nieto, S. (2010). *Language, culture, and teaching: Critical perspectives.* New York, NY: Routledge.

Osborn, T. A. (2006). *Teaching world languages for social justice: A sourcebook of principles and practices.* Mahwah, NJ: Lawrence Erlbaum.

Paris, D. & Alim, H.S. (2017). *Culturally sustaining pedagogies: Teaching and learning for justice in a changing world.* New York, NY: Teachers College Press.

Phillips, J. K. & Abbott, M. (2011). *A decade of foreign language standards: Impact, influence, and future directions.* Retrieved from http://www.actfl.org/sites/default/files/pdfs/public/national-standards-2011.pdf

Reagan, T. G. & Osborn, T. A. (2002). *The foreign language educator in society: Toward a critical pedagogy.* Mahwah, NJ: Lawrence Erlbaum.

Sleeter, C. E. & McLaren, P. L. (1995). Introduction: Exploring connections to build a critical multiculturalism. In C. E. Sleeter & P. L. McLaren (Eds.), *Multicultural education, critical pedagogy, and the politics of difference* (pp. 5-32). Albany, NY: State University of New York Press.

Shrum, J. & Glisan, E.W. (2010) *Teacher's handbook: Contextualized language instruction* (4th Ed.) Boston, MA: Heinle.

Swalwell, K. (2013). *Educating activist allies: Social justice pedagogy with the suburban and urban elite.* New York, NY: Routledge.

Teaching Tolerance. (2016). *Social Justice Standards: The Teaching Tolerance Anti-Bias Framework.* Retrieved from https://www.tolerance.org/sites/default/files/2017-06/TT_Social_Justice_Standards_0.pdf

Wade, R. C. (2007). *Social Studies for social justice.* New York, NY: Teachers College Press.

Wiggins, G. & McTighe, J. (2005). *Understanding by design* (2nd ed.). Alexandria, VA: Assn. for Supervision & Curriculum Development.

CHAPTER 2

Preparing to Teach for Social Justice

Regardless of the type of environment in which you teach, the backgrounds, experiences, abilities, and cultures of every person in your classroom, including you, might lead to very different experiences of social justice education. In this chapter, we will address ways you can build your awareness of your **frame of reference** and those of your students so that a social justice approach can empower you and them. Then, we will provide tools for you to build a learning community that sets the stage for social justice instruction in your world language classroom. In undertaking this work with your students, you will likely coach them through talking about difference or engaging effectively in dialogue with people who may hold different views than they. Therefore, setting the stage for teaching for social justice by understanding yourself and your students, and by creating a safe, comfortable learning environment, is key.

A Glimpse into the Classroom

Laila, a native speaker of Arabic, and Tim, a non-native Japanese speaker, are making strides to include topics of social justice in their world language curricula. Laila teaches novice levels of Arabic in a large, affluent middle school in a metropolitan area. Tim teaches novice and intermediate levels of Japanese in an urban high school where 85% of the students receive free and reduced-priced lunches. Neither teacher has regularly integrated content related to social justice into their curricula, but both have plans to do so this school year.

At the beginning of the year, Laila gave her students a questionnaire about their backgrounds and interests, which she hoped would inform her planning. Currently, she is teaching a unit on food and customs related to eating, and she begins with an interactive lecture about various holidays, such as Ramadan, that influence Muslims' choice of foods in many Arab countries. Laila shares her own personal experiences of observing Ramadan, fasting from sunrise to sunset, and she shares pictures of her family's celebration of Eid al-Fitr at the end of Rama-

dan. During the interactive lecture, Laila gives students reflection questions to draw out some of the information she learned about the students and to help them make connections to the topic.

The first set of reflection questions encouraged students to be able to explain their own perspectives on an important holiday in the Arab world:

- What do you think about Ramadan?

- If you have experience with Ramadan, describe your own perspective on this holiday.

- If you do not have experience with Ramadan, what would be rewarding about it? What might be challenging?

The second set of reflection questions encouraged students to make their own connections to the holiday of Ramadan:

- Think of something to which you had to make a big commitment and see it through. What was it? Why was it important to you?

Meanwhile, in the Japanese classroom of intermediate learners, Tim is also teaching a unit on food and eating customs and plans to focus on *Shin-Okubo*, Korea Town, in Tokyo. While Tim knows most of his students from novice-level classes, he wants to activate their prior knowledge and help them make connections between their own cultural backgrounds and the cultural significance of Koreans, a historically oppressed group, in Japan. He knows his students come from mainly Latino, Hmong, Korean, African American, and East African backgrounds, but he does not know enough about the traditions, beliefs, and interests that are important to them.

Tim's students have notebook journals, and at the beginning of every unit he opts to give his students a short reflection journal assignment to be completed in English or in the target language depending on the complexity of the topic. As preparation for this unit on food, he asks the students to complete a journal assignment about the following questions:

- Name some foods that are important to you and that represent your family and cultural background.

- Why do you eat them and what is the significance of these foods for you?

- What do you know about ethnic communities in our own city?

- What kinds of experiences have you had with the foods in these communities?

Tim collects the journals and reads them as he continues to plan lessons in this unit, integrating opportunities for students to tell their own stories related to food and eating customs.

Now that you have read about these two teachers, please answer these questions:

1. Laila and Tim take various steps to learning more about their students to inform their planning and instruction. What do you think about each of their information-gathering methods? How would you choose to learn more about your students?

2. Examine the types of questions Laila and Tim ask their students. What do you think Laila will learn about her students? What might Tim learn about his?

3. What type of social justice instructional ideas could Laila and Tim develop based on the information they collect in these activities? (Use the categories and activity types that were described in Chapter One to brainstorm ideas.)

Looking into the Mirror: Exploring your Frame of Reference as a Teacher

Our personal frames of reference comprise many aspects of our identities and our experiences. A **frame of reference** is a broader term combining an individual's identity and life experiences, while **identity** refers to how individuals position themselves and identify specific dimensions of themselves. Each of us enters the classroom with unique perspectives about the world that are informed by our ethnicity, sexuality, religion, socioeconomic status, place of origin and current residence, political views, education, age, immigration status, home language(s), and other dimensions.

For example, a pre-service teacher who was raised in a rural, conservative, homogeneous environment might experience challenges in connecting with linguistically and ethnically diverse students in an urban environment. However, a different pre-service teacher, more familiar with her students' frames of reference, might not experience the same challenges. Since teachers' frames of reference have a great influence over how they respond to their students, an exploration of teachers' frames of reference can uncover their biases or stereotypes about approaches to teaching, student learning, and students' identities. Understanding one's own biases or tendency toward certain assumptions or stereotypes is important. Everyone has unexplored beliefs, attitudes, assumptions, and biases, but awareness of them is a critical first step toward creating an equitable classroom and helping students to explore their own biases.

Furthermore, teachers tend to instruct students in the way they themselves were taught—an inclination Lortie (1975) called the **apprenticeship of observation.** For example, if a student in a French class were taught about the French language and culture mostly from a White, European point of view that overlooked Francophone cultures with people of color, such a student, in turn, would commonly become a French teacher who also presents material in a Eurocentric manner. Unfortunately, this approach would not represent the breadth of Francophone cultures and would not connect learning French to the diverse experiences of the students in the class. The teacher did not seek to misrepresent Francophone cultures or marginalize students out of malice; she may have simply taught French in the way that world languages instruction was modeled for her.

By critically examining our frames of reference, we will be better poised to facilitate learning among our students, especially when entering into dialogue about complex topics to which students may react in various ways. In the exercises below, you can explore your own identity and frames of reference and reflect on how you situate yourself in social justice.

Circles of My Multicultural Self
(adapted from www.edchange.org)

Part A: Draw the figure below on a piece of paper. In the middle circle, write your name. In the outside circles, list six (6) descriptors that represent your identity. These can be visible or invisible aspects of your identity.

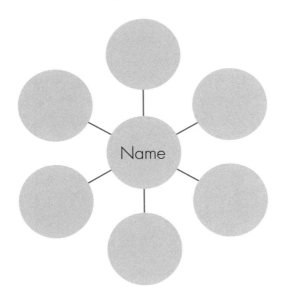

Name

Part B: In light of your graphic, answer the questions below.

1. Think of a time when you were especially proud to be associated with one of your descriptors above. Why was this important to you, and how did it make you feel?

2. Think of a time when an aspect of your identity was interpreted in a negative manner. How did it make you feel to be misunderstood? How did you respond?

3. Name a common stereotype associated with one of the descriptors you identified. I am _____, but I am NOT _____. For example, *I am Muslim, but I am NOT a terrorist.*

Part C: Discuss the answers to the questions below with a partner or a small group.

1. Share a story of pride associated with one of your descriptors with a partner or others in a small group. How did it feel to tell your story? How did others feel to be positively identified with one of their descriptors?

2. If you are comfortable doing so, share your story about a time when someone interpreted one of your descriptors negatively. How did it feel to tell your story this time?

3. Share your stereotype and listen to others share their stereotypes. How would you disrupt the stereotypes you heard others share?

4. Did anyone share a stereotype you have believed or still believe? How are the stereotypes associated with equity, discrimination, or oppression?

Part D: Now that you have explored different facets of your identity through this exercise, take time to reflect on them, and answer these reflection questions related to your culture and your experiences. (Given the sensitive nature of some of these questions in Part D and Part E, you may choose instead to do an individual reflection and a journal entry in response to these questions.) If you are participating in a discussion with others about these questions, please remember that the extent to which you share your answers is completely your choice.

1. Why did you choose to learn another language? How did you learn it?

2. What kinds of traditions are important to you?

3. How are gender and sexuality perceived in your culture?

4. In what way did the socioeconomic status of your family influence opportunities and experiences you had and your view of the world?

5. If you were forced to give up or hide an aspect of your identity, which would you choose? How would this make you feel to not be able to share this part of your identity with others?

Part E: As a final step in this process of exploring your identity, think about what it means for your work in the classroom. Think about how your identity and view of the world may influence your response to various students and to topics that may arise in the classroom.

1. How would you respond if a student in your class brought up an issue related to access or discrimination during a whole group discussion?

2. How might you handle a situation in which one of your students persistently advocates for or against the rights of a specific group?

3. Describe the students to whom you can most relate. Why is it easy for you to understand these students?

4. Describe the students to whom it is hardest for you to relate. Why is it harder for you to understand these students?

Peering into the Classroom: Exploring our Students' Frames of Reference

Sometimes when we talk about "diversity" among our learners, it is easy to immediately equate diversity with students' ethnicities. For example, a student teacher working on his student teaching portfolio wondered how he would address diverse learners, because, as he put it, "All of my students are White." Even in classes where students appear to be racially or ethnically homogeneous, each student has multiple dimensions that make her or him unique: gender, religion, family structure, home language(s), sexual orientation, immigration status, age, and other multifaceted aspects of culture. All of these dimensions, along with students' life experiences, help to shape their frames of reference. Understanding these subtle elements of students' unique identities is a critical first area you must explore before incorporating social justice topics into your world languages curriculum.

In this section, we begin by discussing a few larger categories of student diversity you should consider, including students' cultural backgrounds and abilities. Many of these concepts and activities resonate with the asset-based pedagogies we discussed in Chapter 1, such as **culturally sustaining pedagogy.** Although a more detailed description of enacting culturally relevant pedagogy is beyond the scope of this book, it is foundational to social justice teaching. As a result, we discuss a few key concepts related to culturally sustaining pedagogy to help you form a framework for teaching for social justice in your own classroom.

Students' Backgrounds and Abilities

Students' cultural backgrounds—which can include ethnicity, sexual orientation, gender, socioeconomic status, home language(s), family structure, and other dimensions—greatly inform the way in which they view the world. For example, a heterosexual male student who is cisgender (who presents a gender and personal identity that correspond with his birth sex) may experience access and opportunities in a world language classroom differently than a female or homosexual male student. Students gain a variety of experiences due to their cultural backgrounds, and they will respond to social justice curriculum in different ways, particularly if they have experienced privilege or have encountered marginalization (Swalwell, 2013).

As discussed earlier, in an equitable classroom the teacher recognizes that some students require more scaffolding or different types of academic or emotional support to succeed. Students therefore enter the classroom with a range of abilities and needs. In many inclusive classrooms, students may need additional supports for academic success that are detailed in their Individual Educational Plans (IEP) or 504 Plans. Others may need less scaffolding and more independence in their learning. However, in an equitable classroom, teachers respond to students' needs that extend beyond ability levels, often providing a variety of strategies and support for their students. For example, under Title IX, students are protected from discrimination or harassment based on gender. Students who are struggling with these aspects of their identities may require additional emotional support to succeed academically in the classroom.

(For more information, please see Chapter 7, where we provide a brief overview of the main principles of differentiation, and how they align with the objectives of teaching for social justice. These principles can be applied to all world language classrooms in order to respond appropriately to students' frames of reference, backgrounds and unique needs.)

Drawing on Students' Assets

All students enter into the learning process with **cultural capital** specific to each individual. The notion of cultural capital was first theorized by Pierre Bourdieu (1977) to describe how certain cultural knowledge influences opportunities for achievement and success. He posited that cultural capital is passed down through communities and one's family. This cultural capital is typically connected to one's social class and is manifest in one's tastes, clothes, skills, possessions, and credentials. Bourdieu's theory has continued to be used in educational contexts to describe the unique knowledge and view of the world each student possesses. Typically, students who are not part of the dominant culture or are from a lower SES have experienced a devaluation of their cultural capital.

However, to tap into students' assets and value all types of cultural capital, teachers must consider the danger in such statements as "I don't see color." When teachers claim not to see color, they are essentially refusing to acknowledge key elements of their students' identities. Additionally, we believe this statement is, in and of itself, a microaggression. Although Tatum (1999) notes that it feels wrong for teachers to state that they see racial and ethnic differences in their students, she urges teachers to adopt a color-conscious view of students in the classroom, enabling teachers to draw on the unique strengths the students' racial and cultural background bring into the learning experience. Since Tatum's original work almost two decades ago, many other researchers, scholars, and educators have advocated for doing away with the counterproductive colorblind approach to educating students, yet there is still a stance of colorblindness among educators in schools. We urge you to think critically about the implications of colorblindness and to truly see the students before you.

Finally, it is important to develop a culturally sustaining pedagogy (CSP) and inclusive environment focused on sustaining cultural and linguistic backgrounds of students in the classroom. Paris & Alim (2014) argue that CSP requires a link to social justice and change in a way that previous asset pedagogies have not, and that a push for CSP is vital, given the pervasive value placed on monoculturalism and monolingualism in the United States. The ability to speak dominant American English (DAE), and to retain multiple ways of speaking in students' own communities and beyond, should be considered an advantage, not a disadvantage, as those who view DAE as the main path to success and power (Paris & Alim, 2014). In the context of world language, that means we are uniquely poised to sustain and affirm students' own languages and cultures while allowing them to explore new languages and cultures, adding to the richness of the work we already do as language teachers.

Well before CSP entered our vocabulary, a case study of ten African-American students in an urban middle school setting showed that sustaining students' cultural and linguistic backgrounds while teaching them a new language (Arabic) was effective. The teacher used students' L1—African-American English Vernacular (AAEV)—to facilitate their acquisition of Arabic. Additionally, students' own cultures were regularly integrated into the lessons and teaching, leading to the students feeling valued (Moore & English, 1998). As our classrooms become more diverse and students arrive at schools with a variety of cultural and linguistic backgrounds, it is necessary to draw on the assets of these backgrounds and explore less dominant cultural and linguistic backgrounds in the target cultures.

Ensure that All Students are Represented

A study that explored the topic of belonging among 5,494 White, Asian-American, African-American and Latino students in seven ethnically diverse high schools points to a high correlation among belonging, motivation, and academic success. The study underscores that students can feel connected to school in a variety of ways, and because of these various avenues to belonging that include relationships with peers and teachers, lack of ethnic-based discrimination, and involvement, schools must seek a range of strategies to help students feel a sense of belonging (Faircloth & Hamm, 2005).

Finally, in a study of heritage learners in a Spanish for heritage learners class, the resistant "learners were most responsive to tasks and projects that were 'real,' that is, learning that came from personal or direct experiences, emerging from student interests—not from material transmitted to students without acknowledging and tapping into their own expertise and experience" (Helmer, 2011, p. 139). These studies underscore the importance of designing curriculum that represents and values all students in the classroom, engaging in instruction that gives all students a voice, creating a safe, welcoming environment, and building strong relationships with all students.

Unfortunately, world language classrooms, like many classrooms in schools, do not always ensure that every student is represented or given a voice. Krishauna Hines-Gaither, a college-level Spanish instructor in North Carolina, suggests that world language classrooms may not always be inclusive for diverse learners: "In my experience, world language educators can, at times, create spaces that appear alienating to students… Languages are presented as if they are for a select few who possess the innate abilities necessary to pursue language study." Historically, language learning has had a Eurocentric bias and has been treated as an elitist course of study with enrollment tending to be affected by the social class background of students, i.e., more middle-to-upper-class students (Reagan & Osborn, 2002). It is plausible that students' decisions to opt in or out of language study are influenced by "sociopolitical power relationships" and the choice of language to study may be influenced by students' own perceptions of their abilities, backgrounds, and future opportunities (Reagan & Osborn, 2002, p. 4).

Furthermore, students come to the language classroom with a variety of linguistic experiences, some positive, some painful. Woodley (2016) points out that some students' home languages have been fraught with pain, being given labels of "improper," "not standard," "poor," "other," or "broken" (p. 572). She suggests that we encourage students to tell their own story with language through a myriad of outlets that do not mimic the pain they may have experienced with language learning in the past. Students of diverse backgrounds have stories to tell and voices that should be heard, but traditional language curricula and

instruction conceptualize language-learning in a way that does not focus enough on learning from others or from stories within our own communities (Osborn, 2016), even though every community, including the school community, has voices that need to be heard. Osborn (2016) underscores that "[l]anguage teachers and language teacher educators should become familiar with those stories related to language and develop a critical awareness alongside their students" (p. 569). Incorporating a social justice lens into world language curriculum has the potential to not only push teachers toward meeting the needs of students of varied abilities and backgrounds, but also to highlight voices and stories that have historically been absent from language-learning.

Teaching for social justice extends to all aspects of students' identities. Learning activities must provide opportunities for students to demonstrate their own strengths and knowledge, while also offering scaffolding, options and support for students to account for their unique needs. That is, if equality and equity are both present in the classroom, students have equal access to what they need in order to be successful, but they might take different routes to get there. The fact is, all students need affirmation, respect, inclusion and sensitivity to thrive and succeed, and it is vital to recognize this. However, to include your students in the curriculum in a meaningful way, you must take steps to get to know them and learn about the various aspects of their identities.

In the section below, we recommend three different types of activities that enable you to actively learn about your students. We will also provide some guidelines to help you integrate the information you gather about your students into the curriculum and the learning activities in your classroom. For each activity, we suggest that you create a version based on your own life and interests to share with your students and model the final product. The main objective of taking these steps is to ensure that all of your students are a part of the picture as you develop your curriculum and plan lessons for your students. However, engaging in these kinds of activities within a social justice framework might pressure students to share aspects of themselves that they would prefer not to discuss in class. Creating an environment in which students can feel affirmed and self-actualized is critical and will be discussed later in this chapter.

Your Turn!

Activity 1: Design and Administer a Student Questionnaire

Part A: You will give students a questionnaire to learn more about them. The objective is to gather and make sense of data from students. If you are a pre-service teacher, you could give a questionnaire to a class to which you have access (for example, a field or clinical experience), or you could give it to a world language class on your campus in which the professor and students are willing to participate. In the questionnaire, ask a variety of questions to help you understand the ways students perceive themselves.

The following lists include some possible questions you could use in your questionnaire. Depending on the proficiency level of your students, they could be provided in English, in the target language, or in a combination of both. The types of questions you ask also depend on whether or not the students have been in class with you for a period of time or if they are new to your class. Feel free to adapt the questions to make them more appropriate for your context and grade level, or add questions that are important to you. You should also assure students that they may skip any question they are not comfortable answering.

Some Standard Questions:

1. List three (3) adjectives that best describe who you are. (You could also let students draw themselves or represent their description in another format.)

2. How would you describe your home?

3. How would you describe your family?

4. Which traditions are most important to you and your family?

5. What made you want to learn this language?

6. Describe an aspect of the target culture you find most interesting, and why.

7. What is your greatest strength as a student in our world language class?

8. What is most challenging for you as a student in our world language class?

9. What do you most enjoy about our class?

10. What do you most dislike?

11. Describe a time when you felt that something you learned in our class had a connection to your own life. Please give a specific example.

Some Unique Questions:

1. Would you rather live without your arm or your cell phone? Justify your answer.

2. If you could be a flavor of ice cream, which one would you be, and why?

3. Which food would you choose to have an unlimited supply of, and why?

4. Which animal best represents you? Explain.

5. If you could choose a different name for yourself, which one would you choose? Explain.

6. Would you rather find yourself in _____ (insert book or movie) or in _____ (insert book or movie)? Justify your answer.

7. I was really surprised once when…

8. The best thing I have ever tasted is…

9. The person who understands me best is…

10. The thing that makes me happy when I feel sad is…

Part B: Once you have collected and read through the students' responses, use these questions to help you analyze, interpret, and reflect on the data.

1. What are some overall impressions of the questionnaire that stand out to you?

2. Was there anything about particular students you found surprising or particularly interesting?

3. Were there patterns in aspects of the class students enjoy? In aspects students dislike?

4. Which topics in class did students find most relevant to their own lives? Based on what you know about the students' abilities and cultural backgrounds, did you see any differences or similarities among students?

5. Which aspects of the target culture did students find most interesting? How did students vary in their answers?

6. What did students' answers about their homes, families and traditions tell you about them?

Activity 2: Engage Your Students in an Introductory Project

At the beginning of the course, whether the students are new or returning, introductory projects can reveal a great deal about students' frames of reference.

Often in novice-level classes, students are learning to describe themselves and others, to discuss their interests, and to express preferences. Meanwhile, in intermediate and advanced levels, introductory projects can let students settle into language-learning again, and they can discuss and describe themselves in a more complex manner. This enables teachers to not only engage students in the target language but also gather information about each of their students in a manner less overt than administering a questionnaire. Projects can fit naturally into the curriculum and day-to-day events of the world language classroom. If you have returning students you already know from previous levels, these types of projects can still be useful in reacquainting yourself with each of the students. Furthermore, if students have already developed a relationship with you in a previous class, they may be willing to reveal more information about themselves.

Below you will find several project ideas, but we encourage you to be creative and develop your own project that is catered to the needs of your own classroom. Each of these ideas can be conducted in the target language, may fit well

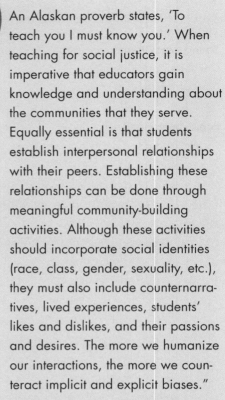

An Alaskan proverb states, 'To teach you I must know you.' When teaching for social justice, it is imperative that educators gain knowledge and understanding about the communities that they serve. Equally essential is that students establish interpersonal relationships with their peers. Establishing these relationships can be done through meaningful community-building activities. Although these activities should incorporate social identities (race, class, gender, sexuality, etc.), they must also include counternarratives, lived experiences, students' likes and dislikes, and their passions and desires. The more we humanize our interactions, the more we counteract implicit and explicit biases."

—Krishauna Hines-Gaither, Greensboro, NC

with technology integration, and are adaptable to a variety of proficiency levels and ages, pre-K through post-secondary.

A. Timeline: Students create a timeline of their lives starting from their birth. However, they should not include other dates on the timeline that correspond to each of their subsequent birthdays. Instead, the pictures and events they include on various points of the timeline should be related to their activities, experiences, interests, people who are important to them, etc. Each of the points on the timeline should correspond to something that has led to the person they are today.

B. Life in Poetry: Students write a poem about themselves, following a specific format that asks them to provide adjectives to describe themselves, express fears, pride, hopes, and identify the people most important to them. Depending on the students' ages or proficiency levels, the language used in these poems can be simplified or altered (Fig. 2.1).

Samuel.	(name)
Young black man.	(what others see when they look at the student)
Creative, funny, artistic.	(3 adjectives that best describe the student)
Brother of Marcus.	(an important relationship: sibling of, friend of, etc.)
Likes hip hop, movies, hanging with friends.	(3 favorite activities)
Feels determined.	(how the student feels about being in world language)
Needs friends, fun, nice teachers.	(3 things the student needs most in school)
Frustrated by bullying and math.	(2 things that frustrates the student)
Is proud to be Sudanese and a friend.	(2 sources of pride for the student)
Looks up to my brother.	(who the student admires most)
Welcome to me.	(a greeting or welcome statement)

Figure 2.1. Life in poetry example

C. Self-Portrait through Pictures: Students compile pictures and write short texts to describe their personalities, appearance, interests, hobbies/activities, family, etc. You can also ask students to identify the characteristics they like the most or of which they are most proud. Students can create their self-portraits in various formats: an interactive poster on Glogster, a collage, a photo album, a Voicethread, or even a blog post. This project is easily adaptable for different ages and proficiency levels.

D. Storytelling: Using no-technology, low-technology or high-technology options, students tell interesting stories about themselves. In a novice-level class, this might be an "all about me" story, using as many nouns, verbs and adjectives as they know to describe themselves. In a class with a higher proficiency level, this might be a story from their childhood or a fun summer adventure story containing various tenses of verbs and more complex vocabulary and sentence structure. This can be done without technology or by using such simple technology tools as Blabberize, Voki, or Fotobabble. These tools allow for creativity, but they also enable students with varied abilities and needs to record and listen to themselves, and to re-record as many times as necessary. Often students who are quiet or shy in class will share more when able to write or record themselves, allowing the teacher to learn more about these students.

Activity 3: Conversation Circles

A teacher can use a number of approaches for conversation circles, but regardless of the approach, it can be useful and insightful for teachers to gather their students as a whole class on a regular basis to engage in spontaneous dialogue around a particular topic. The class forms a circle or semicircle to encourage communication, and depending on the students' comfort and proficiency levels in conversation circle participation, the teacher can allow varying degrees of participation. As the students gain confidence in their abilities to participate in conversation circles, teachers can sit outside of the circle to observe. This gives the learners more agency and control over the discussion, but, as Glisan and Donato (2017) point out, the teacher may need to remain in the circle if students require more scaffolding or if the teacher needs to manage behaviors in a particular class.

One type of conversation circle could involve discussion around an authentic resource students have examined and analyzed in an interpretive task. As the teacher, you would prepare a text-based discussion for students, a high-leverage practice that teaches students the rules for the discussion (i.e., listen carefully, and please don't interrupt others) and preparing them to use gambits (i.e., "I agree with…") (Glisan & Donato, 2017). When you prepare the rules and gambits, consider ones that will ensure that everyone in the class has a fair chance to contribute to and be included in the discussion. You might ask students to follow a rule that requires them to pay attention to their classmates' participation, for instance, by emphasizing that "if some-one has not had the opportunity to speak yet, please invite them to do so." Likewise, you may have to teach students a gambit such as, "____(name), what do you think?" to help them draw each other into the conversation.

In these text-based discussions, Glisan & Donato (2017) suggest that teachers prepare questions about the text ahead of time and post one question at a time for students to discuss, participating only as needed to follow-up on students' statements (i.e., "say more" or "could you explain…"), but avoiding error correction or evaluation of the students' statements. The most important thing you can do is to let the students express their ideas and engage with each other organically and spontaneously in the target language without fear of attention to their mistakes.

In a novice-level classroom, students might complete an interpretive task that asked them to read about the types of after-school activities youth in a target culture engage in, and the conversation circle will focus on allowing students to compare and contrast their own after-school activities with those of the youth in the reading. In examining after-school activities, students can discuss different types of activities youth do, such as taking part in a school sport or clubs, needing to work a part-time job for a variety of reasons, or helping to take care of family.

At a higher proficiency level, the discussion might revolve around a film or novel that contains a topic of social justice, and students are expected to share opinions, provide analysis, and ask thought-provoking questions. This practice of engaging in discussion around a variety of topics and authentic texts will also prepare students to engage with each other when you introduce other topics and texts with themes of social justice, knowing the gambits and norms may vary depending on the theme being covered.

Some Sample Text-Based Discussion Questions

1. What are your responsibilities after school? How are your after-school activities and responsibilities at home similar to or different than the youth in the reading? Why do you think they are similar or different?

[Social justice] has changed the way we view our language experience. Students use the ideas that they learned and explored in French 2 for the social studies classes and for their National Honors Society projects. Students and I connect more now that we have discussed issues that are important to them."

—Catherine Ousselin, French Teacher, Bellingham, WA

2. What do the most frequent after-school activities among youth in _____ culture tell us about what is necessary for them to do or important to them? If youth in _____ work a part-time job to help their families, how is that similar or different to practices in your culture? Why is it similar or different?

3. Which after-school activity is most important to you? Why?

If you do not have a particular authentic resource you want to use as a point of discussion, you may still create conversation circles around topics related to a unit you are teaching. These conversation circles will be geared toward developing an understanding of your students' points of view on a variety of topics that can range from their favorite movies to complex cultural themes. Like text-based discussions, they are conducted primarily in the target language. For example, in a novice level class, the conversation's theme might be "my favorite things," and students share about the things they most like, while other students comment appropriately and ask simple follow-up questions.

Like the text-based discussions, it is important to set up rules and prepare students with gambits they can use to maintain the discussion and engage with their classmates. Depending on the topic and the students' proficiency level, they could be told about the topic ahead of time and asked to prepare questions for their classmates to discuss in the conversation circle. A list of possible questions about the topic could also be generated collaboratively as a class.

If the discussion circle topic is based on an aspect of the target culture, the discussion may or may not take place in the target language, depending on the students' proficiency level.

Some Sample Conversation Circle Questions

1. What is your favorite hobby/music/movie? What is most important about it to you?

2. What makes you happy? What makes you sad?

3. Which hobby or activity would you like to learn? Why?

4. What do you think about the school system in _____ (country)?

5. Do you think you would succeed in this kind of school system? Why or why not?

6. Which students benefit from this kind of system of education? Which students are at a disadvantage under this system of education?

The first time you hold a conversation circle with students new to you, tell them a little about yourself and let them ask questions to learn more about you in either the target language or English, depending on their proficiency level. It is important to create mutual trust by allowing students a glimpse into your world. Finally, use appropriate wait times, and allow for silence. As the teacher, you can prime students (establish norms and lay the groundwork for the discussion activity), allow the question to be posed, and specifically tell students to take a moment to think before sharing, allowing all students to process the question and develop a response (Duckor & Holmberg, 2017) before engaging further in the discussion. This kind of activity builds community and trust, while also allowing students to practice open dialogue with each other, thus laying the groundwork for engaging in discussion about topics of social justice.

Making Space for Students' Identities in Instructional Activities

You may be saying, "Okay, I have learned a lot of information about my students. Now what?" As you do these activities and projects, make notes about characteristics of your students that are key to understanding their iden-tities. You can capitalize on the information you gather about your students in ways that will affirm their identities in your world language class. It also lets you better prepare yourself to teach the diverse students in the class. Below you will find several methods for making space for students' identities in instructional activities.

Give students choices. To give students choices, give them format, topic, and collaboration options. For example, for the self-portrait through pictures project idea, although the learner outcomes for the project would remain the same for all students, they could choose the format for completing the assignment. By doing so, a student interested in creating art could choose to produce his or her self-portrait by hand, while another who enjoys writing or using technology may create a blog. Similarly, by allowing students to choose the topic for a unit, lesson, activity, project, or discussion, they can integrate their frames of reference into the classroom. Letting students choose whether to work individually, with a partner, or in a small group can also help them capitalize on their identities. Although students should learn to work both independently and with others, some work best alone, while others work best collaboratively. Most of all, giving students choices transfers some of the classroom power from teacher to students, giving them agency and control over their own learning. This option also allows students to keep some personal aspects private and does not force them into sharing information that may be difficult to divulge to classmates.

Conduct regular check-ins. By regularly carving out the time (once per month, once each quarter, at the end of each unit, etc.) to gather feedback via short surveys or conversations with students, you can ask them questions related to perceptions of their own progress and make sug-gestions for instruction and learning. Check-ins can take place through paper-and-pencil surveys, online surveys, one-on-one conversations, and whole-group conversa-tions. Using a combination of all of the above lets stu-dents share their voices in different ways and will give the teacher the most insight into ways to approach planning, instruction, and assessment going forward for the whole class and for individuals. Getting to know your students, showing your interest in them, and allowing them to express their opinions demonstrates respect for who they are as individuals and learners. Examples of questions to ask students are:

1. Which learning activities are most effective for you? What kinds of suggestions do you have for learning activities that would be of interest to you?

2. If you could choose the topic for one of our next units, which would you choose?

3. Which topic do you wish we could have spent more time exploring?

4. Which topics have resonated most with you?

5. What suggestions do you have for me to provide a better learning experience for you?

Some of the questions give students voices in the classroom, and if the questionnaire is confidential, students hesitant to share their answers with their teacher one-on-one may feel comfortable providing candid responses in a questionnaire. Some of these questions can enable you to reflect on your practice as well. (The process of reflection will be discussed in further detail in Chapter 6.)

Represent students' identities in examples. Having gathered information on your students through questionnaires, projects and discussions, you can also compare and contrast their identities with the ways people of the target culture and topics are represented in the classroom. As students look around your classroom, they should be able to see themselves, whether in a store-bought poster or in student-created posters and artwork. (Chapter 8 offers more suggestions for how to do this.) Representing your students also extends to classroom procedures and activities. For example, if most examples of cultural products, practices, and perspectives are Eurocentric in nature or representative of only able-bodied people, the topics will have less meaning and relevance for students of diverse backgrounds or students with disabilities. Including themes and activities that represents students' interests, abilities, and backgrounds is a key way to affirm your students' identities.

Building Learning Communities that Bridge Differences

The next stage of preparation to teach for social justice is all about building a learning community in your world language classroom. Luzbette Russo of Fairless Hills, Pennsylvania, questions how she can adequately prepare students to engage in socially sensitive topics, a common question for teachers as they explore how to incorporate social justice understandings into their curricula. In this section, we describe steps you can take to affirm student identities, build a strong learning community in your classroom, and create an environment in which students can feel comfortable exploring more complex topics.

As a teacher, some key points need consideration as you bring your students together in a diverse learning community. The world language classroom can be transformed into a place in which students participate in language and cultural activities, but also in which their identities are affirmed as they gain deeper understandings of products, practices and perspectives of the target culture(s).

Many of us recall a schooling experience in which we felt uncomfortable, stressed, disenfranchised, or disempowered. Can you imagine engaging in an activity or participating in a discussion about a sensitive topic in that type of environment? In their *Toolkit for Tongue-Tied*, Teaching Tolerance (2014) provides a number of "critical practices" teachers can use when discussing sensitive topics. They note, "Social emotional learning, respect and safety are as important as literacy and critical thinking skills… Research shows that students need to feel both physically and emotionally safe to learn. This includes safety from stereotype threat, harassment and exclusion."

Teachers must create warm, nurturing spaces in which students feel comfortable, confident, and willing to participate. This is even more critical when teachers plan to teach about social justice issues in their lessons. Creating such a space involves thinking carefully about the specific **teacher practices** you engage in (what you do as a teacher during lessons) and the **dispositions** you embody toward your learners (your attitudes, beliefs and how they manifest in your actions). These practices and dispositions include how you build trust and community, how you set up classroom routines, how you engage with students outside the classroom, and the conscious and unconscious practices you use in your lesson-planning and instruction.

Here are some key ways to prepare to support students for critical engagement in your social justice activities:

Capitalize on your students' unique perspectives. Make the most of what you learned about students' backgrounds and contexts. Their frames of reference can provide a great deal of richness in the process of learning and engaging in dialogue about complex aspects of culture in language classrooms. Allow students options and some freedom in their learning activities and demonstration of their understanding. By doing so, you will find that students' abilities and perspectives on the world become more apparent, which will aid you in linking the target language and culture to relevant aspects of the students' own lives.

Nieto (2010) suggests that teachers act as a bridge for their students to connect students' differences to the dominant culture. This notion can be applied in multiple ways as we think about teaching for social justice in world language classrooms. First of all, a bridge can bring students together and let them view topics from different perspectives found both within and outside of the classroom. Secondly, a bridge can guide all students on a journey from their own culture to the target culture(s) studied in class. One of the best characteristics of a bridge is that the value of it increases over time because students coming from different sides of the bridge can use it to understand various viewpoints and contexts (Nieto, 2010).

Be a facilitator, and actively engage the students. hooks (1994) reminds us that a teacher is not supposed to just deliver information, but to be a "catalyst" to draw students into the dialogue and learning process (p. 11). Students should be active participants. In *Pedagogy of the Oppressed,* Freire (1993) referred to the traditional approach to education as a "banking" model of education, in which the teacher possesses all of the knowledge and fills students with it as though they are empty receptacles (p. 72). For example, the students sit silently, the teacher gives them discrete points of information, and in many cases in banking education, the students are expected to recall

these discrete points on assessments such as worksheets, quizzes, and tests. We implore you to move beyond this model by using activities that allow students to make sense of the content in their own ways and through the use of critical thinking skills. The development of critical thinking skills can be one of the long-lasting benefits of social justice education, but it cannot take place unless the teacher is willing to help students become "agents of their own learning" (Nieto, 2010, p. 189) and use what they learn in a meaningful way. This knowledge and learning is reflected in authentic performance assessments, discussed further in Chapters 3 and 4.

Create a discourse community that encourages discussion. In a discourse community, interpersonal conversation between the teacher and student and among students is encouraged and nurtured through meaningful topics (Glisan & Donato, 2017). For example, when students enter the classroom, engaging in dialogue right away with them about relevant topics is one way to begin a discourse community in the classroom. Asking students in the target language how their game was the night before, how their morning is going, what they have planned for the weekend, etc., develops not only relationships with the students but also their confidence in using the target language.

Glisan and Donato (2017) recommend the high-leverage teaching practice of Initiate Response Feedback (IRF), in which teachers do not simply evaluate what students say, but provide feedback. The teacher initiates conversation, the student responds, and the teacher comments on the student's response. For example, the teacher asks a student, "How was your game last night?" and the student responds, "It was good." Rather than evaluating the student's response as correct or incorrect, the teacher engages the student further: "I'm glad to hear that. Who won?" This continues the conversation further. These interpersonal interactions should take place daily in the classroom, and they will carry over to more complex discussions around social justice issues. This will allow the teacher, for example, to initiate discussion by saying, "I thought we might start today by discussing the recent event that took place last night in our community. What are your reactions to it?" and giving feedback such as, "Tell me more. Why do you think that?" after students respond. The development of a discourse community can allow students to develop communicative skills and proficiency while discussing social justice issues, making it possible for the teacher to engage novice learners through advanced learners in a wide variety of meaningful topics.

Be courageous and challenge students with topics and action. World language teachers are in the position to take a stand on issues related to equity and to help students examine and discuss these issues. According to Freire: "No teacher is worth her salt who is not able to confront students with a rigorous body of knowledge…" (Kincheloe, 2007, p. 21). Naturally, it is safer and easier to engage students in discussions of superficial topics of culture, but doing so does not allow students to gain an authentic understanding of the lives of others, one of the most important components of world language instruction. To peer below the surface of the products of culture to explore practices and perspectives, the teacher must invite the students to view the culture through different lenses and to employ critical thinking skills. Once you have decided to challenge your students with more rigorous topics, you must clarify your intentions (hooks, 1994), as students need to understand the philosophy underlying the practice of exploring and discussing topics of social justice.

After students have engaged in a topic of social justice, world language teachers are also in the position to challenge their students to act. In an advanced-level Spanish course Joan Clifford teaches at Duke University, an opportunity for her students to work toward understanding and change presented itself. Her students partnered with the County Public Health Department (CPHD) to disseminate the results of their yearly survey and to hold focus groups with the members of the Spanish-speaking community. Clifford prepared her students by facilitating an understanding of the Latino population in their area, and a local Latino community organizer coached the students. The other activity Clifford required before engaging in the research project with CPHD was attendance at an event in the community to observe various interactions and learn more about organizations they would visit. In collaboration with the CPHD, the students were able to deliver survey results to members of the Spanish-speaking community and elicit feedback through group information

sessions and one-on-one conversations. Clifford asserts that this project allowed students to develop a critical consciousness about service to diverse communities, social determinants of health, and the need for more multilingual staff in local institutions. Such an opportunity could give students the knowledge and confidence to act on their own in the future when they see occasions to work toward social justice in a variety of contexts.

Be okay with silence. The content of social justice lessons is not as neutral as many language-focused ones. As a result, you might find it challenging to start discussions about social justice issues. At times, students may not feel comfortable answering questions or voicing their perspectives on a given topic. In her work on silence in the classroom, Schultz (2009) redefines classroom participation to include both engaged silence and multimodal responses. In addition, she notes that silence has the potential to communicate other messages, including resistance, boredom, or thoughtfulness. As teachers, we must be responsive to silence and willing to "check-up" on students' emotional responses to the content, to their work in their classroom, and to the general classroom dynamics. Finally, you will need to empathize with and support the complex emotions and responses from students that may emerge.

Many of these practices stretch beyond the specifics you will plan for a given lesson, but you must consider them daily if you incorporate social justice understandings into your curriculum. Ultimately, you will weave these practices together to create a larger approach to teaching world languages that guides your daily planning and enactment of lessons.

Conclusion

In this chapter, we invited you to consider your own identity and the way in which your frame of reference influences the way you approach students, instruction and learning. We hope you have begun to reflect on your own background and your positioning in social justice so you can think about how to most effectively engage with students in social justice topics. The process of reflection is ongoing and will be discussed further in Chapter 6. Additionally, you learned about your students' identities through different activities and to think about steps you can take to integrate their identities into the curriculum, teaching and learning. Finally, you contemplated how to bridge your identity and the varied identities of your students together to create a sense of community in your world language classroom. Ensuring that every student is a part of the picture will put you on the path to creating successful learning experiences based in social justice for your world language students.

Discussion Questions

1. Which characteristics do you value most in your students? How do you react when students lack those characteristics? What steps do you take to engage with those students effectively?

2. Think of a time when a student's ability or unique knowledge on a certain topic surprised you. If you are a pre-service teacher, perhaps you can think of a student you met in a clinical experience or a fellow student in a class. How could this student's ability or knowledge be used in an effective way in a world language class?

3. With your circles in mind from the Circles of my Multi-cultural Self activity, think about and identify the topics of social justice with which you most struggle. Why do you think these would be hardest? How is the difficulty of these topics connected to aspects of your identity and your frames of reference?

4. Read Peggy McIntosh's article, *White Privilege: Un-packing the Invisible Knapsack*, accessible online (see references). In what way do you believe that you have benefited from unearned privilege, or in what way have you experienced marginalization? How might these experiences influence the way in which you view learning and teaching?

REFERENCES

Bourdieu, P. (1977). Cultural reproduction and social reproduction, in J. Karabel & A. H. Halsey (Eds.), *Power and Ideology in Education* (pp. 487-511). New York, NY: Oxford University Press.

Bourdieu, P. (1986). The forms of capital. In J. G. Richardson (Ed.), *Handbook of theory and research for the sociology of education* (pp. 241-248). New York, NY: Greenwood Press.

Duckor, B. & Holmberg, C. (2017). *Mastering formative assessment moves: Seven high-leverage practices to advance student learning.* Alexandria, VA: ASCD.

Faircloth, B. & Hamm, J. (2005). Sense of belonging among high school students representing four ethnic groups. *Journal of Youth and Adolescence, 34*(4), 293-309.

Freire, P. (1993). *Pedagogy of the oppressed* (2nd ed.). New York, NY: The Continuum Publishing Group.

Gay, G. (2002). Preparing for culturally responsive teaching. *Journal of Teacher Education, 53*(2), 106-116.

Glisan, E. W. & Donato, R. (2017). *Enacting the work of language instruction: High-leverage teaching practices.* Alexandria, VA: The American Council on the Teaching of Foreign Languages.

Helmer, K. (2011). "Proper Spanish is a waste of time": Mexican-origin student resistance to learning Spanish as a heritage language. In Scherf, L. & Spector, K. (Eds.), *Culturally relevant pedagogy: Clashes and confrontations* (135-164). Plymouth, UK: Rowman & Littlefield Education.

hooks, b. (1994). *Teaching to transgress: Education as the practice of freedom.* Boston, MA: South End.

Kincheloe, J. (2004). *Critical pedagogy.* New York, NY: Peter Lang Publishing, Inc.

Lortie, D. (1975). *Schoolteacher: A sociological study.* London, UK: University of Chicago Press.

McIntosh, P. (1989). White privilege: unpacking the invisible knapsack. *Peace and Freedom Magazine,* July/August, p. 10-12. Retrieved from: https://nationalseedproject.org/white-privilege-unpacking-the-invisible-knapsack

Moore, Z. T. & English, M. (1998). Successful teaching strategies: Findings from a case study of middle school African-Americans learning Arabic. *Foreign Language Annals, 31*(3), 347-357.

Nieto, S. (2010). *Language, culture, and teaching: A critical perspective.* New York, NY: Routledge.

Osborn, T. (2016). Architects wanted for professional remodeling: A response to Ennser-Kananen. *Modern Language Journal,* 100, 568-570.

Paris, D. & Alim, H. S. (2014). What are we seeking to sustain through culturally sustaining pedagogy? A loving critique forward. *Harvard Educational Review, 84*(1), 85-100.

Reagan, T. G. & Osborn, T. A. (2002). *The foreign language educator in society: toward a critical pedagogy.* Mahwah, NJ: Lawrence Erlbaum Associates, Inc.

Schulz, K. (2009). *Rethinking classroom participation: Listening to silent voices.* New York, NY: Teachers College Press.

Swalwell, K. (2013). *Educating activist allies: Social justice pedagogy with the suburban and urban elite.* New York, NY: Routledge.

Tan, E., & Calabrese Barton, A. (2012). *Empowering science and mathematics education in urban schools.* Chicago, IL: University of Chicago Press.

Tatum, B. D. (1997). *Why are all the Black kids sitting together in the cafeteria?* New York, NY: Basic Books.

Teaching Tolerance. (2018). Examining identity and assimilation. Retrieved from: https://www.tolerance.org/classroom-resources/tolerance-lessons/examining-identity-and-assimilation

Teaching Tolerance. (2014). Toolkit for tongue-tied. *Teaching Tolerance,* 46. Retrieved from: https://www.tolerance.org/magazine/spring-2014/toolkit-for-tonguetied

Woodley, H. (2016). From pain to healing in language teacher education. *Modern Language Journal,* 100, 570-572.

CHAPTER 3
Creating Original Social Justice Units

This chapter will guide you in creating original, communication-based units that are connected at a fundamental level with important principles in social justice education. If you are a pre-service teacher, this will enable you to think about big-picture planning, including the standards that guide our instruction, the social justice and language goals you plan, and the authentic, summative assessment you use at the end of the unit. If you are an in-service teacher, this chapter will enable you to think deeply about the alignment between your long-range planning and your incorporation of social justice themes and understandings.

A Glimpse into the Classroom

It's a new school year at Franklin High. Li, Elena, and three of their colleagues—French teacher Ayana, Spanish teacher William, Arabic teacher Samira—have the opportunity to collaboratively plan their first unit in their novice-level world languages classes. This year, Dr. Rodríguez-Durand, their department supervisor, has given them three days during their district's end-of-summer pre-planning session to create the unit and plan their lessons for the first few weeks of the school year.

Li and Ayana participated in a professional development session last spring at their regional foreign language conference on incorporating social justice understandings into world languages curricula. After the conference, they worked with their colleagues to create a structure for an introductory unit adaptable to their specific target languages and cultures. On the first day of pre-planning, they began with an identity-themed unit, in which students would describe their physical characteristics and personal qualities, tell someone where they are from, and tell someone their age. On a deeper level, they wanted students to explore the connections among personal identity, one's community and one's culture and to examine assumptions and stereotypes related to identity. Li and Ayana thought this would engage students in one of the social justice activities the teachers learned of in the workshop, such as a problem-posing activity or an individual experience investigation.

During their brainstorming session, the teachers talked about some of the stereotypes their high-school students had expressed in past years. The stereotypes were rooted in students' misconceptions about individuals from the target cultures and countries they were studying. For instance, Elena retold an anecdote about one of her ninth-grade students who thought all of the Spanish-speakers in their community were from Mexico. Elena believed that many of her students were unaware of the diversity of cultures within the Spanish-speaking community and did not realize that their understandings of Spanish-speakers were based largely on stereotypical images. Samira also talked about some of the racist and prejudiced statements she had heard from some of her students. William then thought of an understanding that would be applicable despite their target language or culture: "Our identities are multifaceted, intersectional, and connected to experiences and membership in different social groups." This aligned well with the *Social Justice Standards* Identity Anchor Standards (Teaching Tolerance, 2016).

As a team, the teachers infused the unit with opportunities for their students to explore the various dimensions of their identities, including but not limited to gender, ethnic background, nationality, native language, socioeconomic status, family structure, personality, passions, and life histories. Elena, Li, and their colleagues spent a full day developing a plan for their unit, identifying the target social justice understanding, and creating their summative assessment.

Now that you have read the vignette, answer these questions:

1. What is the basis for the department's unit? How does their decision-making about the unit reflect their students, the teaching context, and their interest in integrating social justice into the curriculum?

2. What misconceptions have your students or others in your community expressed about your target culture(s) or a community who communicates in your target language?

3. What do you think about creating a similar unit to use with your novice-level students? In what way do you think the unit the Franklin HS teachers are planning might be successful in your own classroom? What might you do differently?

Steps in Creating a Social Justice Unit Plan

A unit plan is a long-range plan that typically incorporates several weeks of lessons around a specific theme and a takeaway understanding related to social justice. This type of big-picture planning begins with the basic stages of backward design (Wiggins & McTighe, 2005) and includes three stages (Fig. 3.1).

At this point, we move from these general stages to specific steps that will help you to design an original unit that incorporates social justice. Figure 3.2 shows the steps you will take, and how they provide a bit more detail the

basic stages presented in Chapter 1. As you move through these steps, you may want to use a unit-planning template to stay organized. (See Appendix B for a user-friendly template, or consult the template found in Clementi & Terrill's (2017) *The Keys to Planning for Learning: Effective Curriculum, Unit, and Lesson Design*.)

We also want to encourage you to think about where the unit will fall during the school year, and how it fits with other units you plan to teach. You will also want to consider the logistical aspects of your unit: the number of days you will have to teach it, the length of each instructional period, and other events that will affect your day-to-day instruction.

Step 1: Identify the Theme, an Essential Question, and Social Justice Takeaway Understanding(s) Specify the theme for your unit and the key concepts that will drive it (Fig. 3.3). This will establish a strong foundation for you to articulate learning objectives in the subsequent steps of this process. Envision this theme as an umbrella under which all other pieces of the unit will fit, yet it should be narrow enough to allow students to

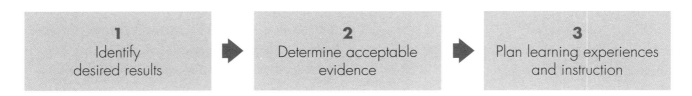

Figure 3.1. Stages of Backward Design (Wiggins & McTighe, 2005)

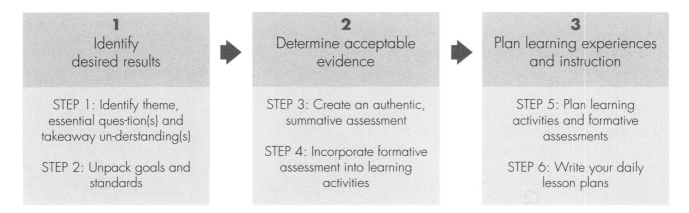

Figure 3.2. Backward Design Stages with Steps for Planning Overlay

> "I am fascinated by a country built on immigration that now builds fences and discusses the possibility of spending billions of dollars on strengthening physical borders with fortified walls. In the classroom, I use the topic of immigration to discuss sympathy and empathy in an effort to have students look closer at the reasons for immigration and to see this as a human rights issue. To drive the point even deeper, most of the lessons/discussions are about migrant children of the same age or younger, with the hopes that we can come as close as we can to empathy for the struggles that these children endure."
>
> — Monica Stillman, Spanish Teacher, Medford, New Jersey

Given our goal of integrating social justice topics into a unit, the theme must allow students to use the language in a real, meaningful way and in a manner leading to critical thinking.

For instance, in the novice-level Chinese example you will see later in this chapter, the teacher chose a theme of *Needs and Wants,* inviting her students to explore their own and others' needs and wants as they relate to specific real-life situations and to examine the work of organizations who address the needs of particular groups of people. In the second example you will view from a post-secondary intermediate level German unit, the theme is *Engaging in Civil Courage.* The students in this unit are asked to read historical and current accounts of acts of civil courage and to consider their own roles as agents of change and their abilities to advocate against acts of injustice. As you will see, this theme will allow the Chinese and German students to develop language skills and cultural knowledge around social justice topics that affect people's daily lives.

After identifying the theme, develop an **essential question** to accompany it. Clementi and Terrill (2017) emphasize that an essential question can help to drive the unit by focusing on the most important content. An essential question should be open-ended, interesting, and even a little provocative. Wiggins and McTighe (2013) assert that essential questions should lead to critical thinking, intellectual engagement, follow-up questions, and justification of one's answer. The authors also acknowledge that world language teachers sometimes struggle with essential questions because language teachers focus on not just content, but also on linguistic nuances (e.g., vocabulary and grammar) that make it more difficult to write an essential

examine "fewer topics in depth rather than many topics superficially," one main benefit of creating a thematic unit (Clementi & Terrill, 2017). Thematic units also lead to more meaningful learning, as language learning remains more contextualized in a thematic unit (Curtain & Dahlberg, 2016; Shrum & Glisan, 2016). Finally, Curtain & Dahlberg (2016) point out, "Thematic planning changes the instructional focus from the language itself to the use of language to achieve meaningful goals," and instruction designed around a theme leads to "complex thinking and more sophisticated use of language" (p. 39).

Identify standards for your unit	Identify the theme of your unit	Identify the social justice take-away understanding

Figure 3.3. Overview of Step 1

question. The authors therefore suggest that world language teachers create broader essential questions (Wiggins & McTighe, 2013). This may allow language teachers to better attend to both language and content.

In the novice secondary Chinese unit, *Needs and Wants,* the essential question is, "What do we need most, and how do we get it?" Meanwhile, the post-secondary intermediate German unit employs an essential question of "How can I speak out and take action?" Note that these questions are broad enough to have not just one right answer, and students can make sense of the question in different ways. This allows students with different abilities, backgrounds, and perspectives to demonstrate their knowledge and ideas in their own ways. For additional ideas, you may want to explore websites that contain lists of essential questions for various content areas, including essential questions for social justice, decisions and consequences, culture, and adversity and change (e.g., TeachThought's *A Giant List of Really Good Essential Questions*).

To identify the **social justice takeaway understanding,** ask yourself: *What are the important understandings*

related to social justice that I want students to be able to take with them as they continue their study of this language and culture(s)? You may have to develop just one key takeaway understanding, or there may be several takeaway understandings you want students to have by the end of the unit. Since you are embedding social justice into the unit, however, these takeaway understandings must reflect the social justice content students will be exploring and investigating.

The takeaway understanding acts as an enduring understanding for the unit and will inform discrete learning points, such as vocabulary and grammar. Additionally, the process of creating this takeaway understanding will help you to clarify the important ideas related to social justice students will encounter throughout the unit. The knowledge students gain should extend beyond this unit; like the essential question, the understanding should be broad enough to explore a few different topics yet narrow enough to focus on a particular social justice issue and its related topics.

For example, in the novice Chinese unit the social justice takeaway understanding is, "Although helping others in need is important, successful action takes place not by being a 'savior,' but by empowering those in need through sustainable practices that support them to help each other." The intermediate German unit contains multiple social justice takeaway understandings: "(1) Civil courage can be enacted in big and small ways; (2) Individuals can make a difference by advocating for the rights of others; and (3) A person's ability to carry out civil courage can vary based on their background and own experiences." The takeaway understandings in both example units let the teacher emphasize steps for action, one of Hackman's (2005) five components of social justice education. Both also emphasize an understanding of how students can engage in service in an appropriate, responsive way or to advocate for those whose rights are being infringed upon.

> " Most of my students, despite their young age, are able to truly understand my unit's essential questions about what they believe is fair or not, and how we can "fix" things they decide are not so just around the world. The questions I have heard from my students are big questions that allow them to think critically and to embrace their role as world citizens. These questions show they are capable of thinking of others not so much as people who live far away or who are different because they speak a different language, but rather as part of a larger community that we all share."
>
> — Madji Fall, Glassboro, New Jersey

Your Turn!

Before we go any further, it is your turn to identify your theme, essential question(s), and social justice takeaway understanding(s). It is important to feel confident about these pieces, as they will greatly inform the other details of the unit. For assistance in this process, refer back to the descriptions of Step 1 and the Chinese and German examples above.

Theme and Essential Question
Social Justice Takeaway Understanding(s)

Step 2: Unpack Standards and Unit Goals

Start by consulting the *World-Readiness Standards for Foreign Language Learning* (The National Standards Collaborative Board, 2015) and your state or institutional standards for world languages. Also review Teaching Tolerance's *Social Justice Standards* (2016), which provide anchor standards and learning outcomes specific to social justice content for P-12 students. These sets of standards should ground the unit by providing the overarching goals for what your students will know and be able to do based on their proficiency levels and grade clusters. Note that the *World-Readiness Standards* are content standards and provide only a general direction for your students' learning; they are not a curriculum guide and do not provide a scope and sequence (Shrum & Glisan, 2016). Also consult the *NCSSFL-ACTFL Can-Do Statements* (NCSSFL-ACTFL, 2017) and state and local frameworks (Shrum & Glisan, 2016). Many state standard frameworks are organized as performance standards, which may also be called benchmarks, performance outcomes, student learning objectives, or another term that suggests *what* the students should be able to do or communicate with the language, and in some cases, *how well.*

The *NCSSFL-ACTFL Can-Do Statements* (NCSSFL-ACTFL, 2017) provide clear, user-friendly global benchmarks for intercultural communication organized by mode of communication, but with benchmarks and performance indicators for intercultural communication as well. For example, the *Can-Do* performance indicator for novice-level learners in their ability to identify practices states: "In my own and other cultures, I can identify some typical practices related to everyday life." Having a good sense of how students can build their intercultural communicative competence at their specific proficiency levels will be essential as you write unit goals.

Regarding the culture standards, as outlined in Chapter 1, social justice issues in the world language classroom belong to one of three categories, overlapping with how culture is defined and organized in the *World-Readiness Standards* (The National Standards Collaborative Board, 2015):

1. **Products:** social justice issues that focus on access to and relationships with tangible and intangible resources.

2. **Practices:** social justice issues that arise from how people interact.

3. **Perspectives:** social justice issues stemming from attitudes, beliefs and values.

We do not recommend that teachers try to isolate social justice topics into just one of these three categories. Rather, we encourage you to see how all social justice issues ultimately relate to and reflect perspectives, even if the emphasis might initially be on issues related more to products or practices. For example, in connection with the Chinese unit, *Needs and Wants,* although the focus may seem to be on tangible and intangible products one may need or want, cultural perspectives underlie these products. As students identify the needs of particular groups, for example, they can explore the perspectives underlying the way in which Chinese and American organizations help individuals or groups in need.

Ultimately, **unit goals** should be written for students, not for teachers; they *should not* communicate what you, as the teacher, will do during the lesson. The unit goals should point to what learners will know and will be able to do by the end of the unit and should not be focused on particular vocabulary or grammar students will need to know to succeed in the unit (Clementi & Terrill, 2017). The specific language students will need in the unit will become apparent after you have identified the summative assessments in the next step and key formative assessments (Chapter 5). The unit goals must reflect a variety of lower-order and higher-order thinking skills; to succeed in the unit, students will need to engage in a range of thinking and skills. After you write the goals, examine them again to ask yourself: "How do these goals bring together social justice content, language, and culture?" The unit goals allow students to develop knowledge and skills in a real-world, meaningful manner (see Tables 3.1 and 3.2).

> " During a second grade (novice-low) unit on 'The World Cup,' students learn how to ask and answer where they are from, where their parents are from, where famous soccer players are from, the seven continents, and the countries and flags of participating teams. To tie in social justice, my students are shocked to learn that 67 million children in the world do not have access to an education, more than all children in primary school in the US, Europe, Canada, and Australia combined. However, the World Cup has the power of uniting nations around the world around one passion: soccer. Students learn about how singer Shakira, the 'footballers,' and the Fédération Internationale de Football Association (FIFA) teamed up during the 2010 World Cup to support the 1Goal: Education for All campaign, which works to ensure that every child in the world gets a safe, free, and quality education."
>
> —Mary Devine, Haddon Heights, New Jersey

Your Turn!

Now it is your turn to unpack the World-Readiness Standards (The National Standards Collaborative Board, 2015), Social Justice Standards (Teaching Tolerance, 2017), and state or other standards, if appropriate, and to develop the unit's goals. Remember that you will address all three of the Communication Standards through your summative and formative assessments, but you might provide some evidence of how other standards will be met. Note that your goals should lead students to both the essential question(s) and social justice takeaway understanding(s), thus should encompass the social justice topic(s) you have embedded in the unit.

Goals		
World Readiness Standards		
Communication: • Interpersonal, Interpretive, Presentational		
Teaching Tolerance Social Justice Standards		
Other Standards (optional)		
Social Justice Activity Types		

Step 3: Develop a Summative Authentic Assessment

This assessment, which you will use at the end of the unit, will help to determine how well students have met the overarching objectives you identified for this unit.

A **summative assessment** occurs at the end or after a unit and enables you to determine the students' progress to-

Table 3.1. Novice High Level Chinese Unit Goals and Standards (Unit Written by Reed Riggs)

Goals

- Students will be able to request and obtain things they need and want in hotels, homestays, and restaurants.

- Students will be able to identify the difference between needs and wants in their own daily lives and in the lives of others in both the U.S. and in China.

- Students will be able to describe one Chinese organization that helps Chinese people in need (where, who and how they help) and one US organization that helps American people in need.

- Students will be able to compare and contrast the role of and the type of help provided by the Chinese and the American organizations.

World-Readiness Standards	Teaching Tolerance Social Justice Standards
Communication: • Interpersonal, Interpretive, Presentational **Cultures:** • Practices to Perspectives: Staying in a hotel or with a family in China; eating in Chinese restaurants; practices of domestic aid organizations • Products to Perspectives: Chinese hotels; Chinese homes; Chinese restaurants; products from domestic aid organizations **Connections:** • Making Connections: Social studies and understanding lives of people in China • Acquiring Information and Diverse Perspectives: • Text from domestic aid organizations in China **Comparisons:** • Language Comparisons: Use of reference words like this, that, here; there; descriptions using names, numbers, places • Cultural Comparisons: Comparisons of needs and wants in China versus U.S. in different contexts—in homes, in hotels, in restaurants; domestic aid organizations in U.S. versus China—Who is in need? What do they need? **Communities:** • School and Global Communities: Recognition and identification of needs and wants within their own school and communities • Lifelong Learning: Ability to understand typical practices when traveling in China	**Diversity:** • Students will develop language and knowledge to ac-curately and respectfully describe how people (including themselves) are both similar to and different from each other and others in their identity groups. **Justice:** • Students will recognize that power and privilege influence relationships on interpersonal, intergroup and institutional levels and consider how they have been affected by those dynamics.

Table 3.2. Intermediate Low Level German Unit Goals and Standards

Goals

- Students will know that resistance movements throughout history have been carried out by citizens who have felt called to act against injustice.

- Students will be able to compare and contrast various acts of civil courage, both small and large.

- Students will be able to explain steps they can take toward action in certain situations.

- Students will be able to describe their own point of view and others' perspectives regarding injustices and action that may be necessary.

World-Readiness Standards

Communication:
- Interpersonal, Interpretive, Presentational

Cultures:

- Practices to Perspectives: Acts of civil courage among different groups of citizens

- Products to Perspectives: Various authentic texts put out by groups advocating for civil courage (leaflets, social media, videos, images)

Connections:

- Making Connections: Historical resistance movements such as Nazi resistance groups during WWII

- Acquiring Information and Diverse Perspectives: Leaflets written by Nazi resistance groups and other authentic texts; sites of resistance through virtual field trips

Comparisons:

- Language Comparisons: Use of subjunctive in English and in German

- Cultural Comparisons: Historical acts of resistance and civil courage in German and the U.S. (Nazi resistance, Civil Rights Movement) and more current acts of resistance and civil courage in both countries (Women's March; #MeToo; Anti-Nazi; Anti-Pegida – Patriotic Europeans Against the Islamisation of the West)

Communities:

- School and Global Communities: Ways in which stu-dents can engage in small acts of civil courage, both within and outside of their college communities

- Lifelong Learning: Understanding how and when to take action

Teaching Tolerance Social Justice Standards

Justice:

- Students will recognize unfairness on the individual level (e.g., biased speech) and injustice at the institutional or systemic level (e.g., discrimination).

- Students will analyze the harmful impact of bias and injustice on the world, historically and today.

Action:

- Students will express empathy when people are excluded or mistreated because of their identities and concern when they themselves experience bias.

- Students will recognize their own responsibility to stand up to exclusion, prejudice and injustice.

- Students will speak up with courage and respect when they or someone else has been hurt or wronged by bias.

- Students will make principled decisions about when and how to take a stand against bias and injustice in their everyday lives and will do so despite negative peer or group pressure.

ward the objectives you articulated. It can also enable you to communicate those results to the students, families, or other stakeholders the school (Kelly Hall, 2001). It should provide the evidence that students have learned what you intended (Wiggins & McTighe, 2006).

An **authentic assessment** allows students to engage in tasks similar to real life experiences they could have outside of the classroom (Shrum & Glisan, 2016). Authentic assessments also allow teachers to examine each individual student's performance and depth of knowledge in a way that a traditional assessment, like a test, rarely can. Not all summative assessments are authentic (e.g., a test), and not all authentic assessments are summative (e.g., an informal role play during a class), but original social justice units should include at least one assessment that is both summative and authentic and, ideally, allows students to demonstrate knowledge about a social justice issue or topic explored in the unit.

As you begin to think about your unit's summative authentic assessment, ask yourself:

- What would students need to show me *at the end of the unit* for me to be confident that all of my goals have been met?

- How would that evidence translate into an assessment that would *integrate the modes of communication and social justice understandings?*

- How could I make this assessment *authentic,* using real-world tasks students could perform in real life?

The framework for a summative, authentic assessment we use is the *Integrated Performance Assessment* (IPA) (Adair-Hauck, Glisan, & Troyan, 2013; Sandrock, 2010), which enables students to demonstrate their knowledge and proficiency through all three modes of communication: interpretive, interpersonal, presentational (Adair-Hauck et al., 2013).

The IPA's first task is interpretive, such as reading a text or watching a video. Clementi and Terrill (2017) suggest creating several interpretive tasks to address various aspects of interpretive communication—reading, listen-

A few of the assessment options that I provide to assess their understanding are: (1) essay writing; (2) performance assessments (role-play, rehearsed or improvised/spontaneous skits); (3) educational technology projects, such as creating and publishing a website or creating a mobile app in order to raise awareness of the identified and understood issue and to explore possible action steps; (4) PowerPoint or Prezi presentations of the genesis and reality of the issue and proposed steps to address and solve the issue."

— Richard de Meij, Hartford, Connecticut

ing, viewing. In the German unit, for example, students could listen to a song with the theme of resistance or civil courage, watch a short video about individuals engaging in *Zivilcourage* on YouTube, and read an authentic text on social media from various groups and individuals. Students complete a comprehension guide that should ask them to interpret the text in both a literal and an interpretive manner (Adair-Hauck, Glisan, & Troyan, 2013). Shrum & Glisan (2016) assert that, when students use their native language to answer questions during interpretive tasks, they demonstrate a deeper understanding of what they have read, listened to, or viewed.

After receiving explicit teacher feedback via a rubric on their work in the interpretive tasks, the students then complete a related interpersonal task (e.g., an interview or a conversation with another student). Finally, after explicit teacher feedback on the interpersonal task, they build on their work in the prior two tasks to complete the presentational task. Sometimes it is desirable to complete the presentational task before the interpersonal task, depending on the context of the assessments.

Figure 3.4 provides an example IPA overview and task descriptions for the Novice Level Chinese and Intermediate Level German units. Notice how both incorporate social justice themes.

Example 1: Novice High Level Chinese Unit, Written by Reed Riggs

Needs and Wants

OVERVIEW: Students complete tasks that require them to examine the needs of various groups and individuals and to both request what they need and to reflect on their own needs and wants.

Interpretive Tasks:

Students examine infographics about groups in need and rank them from most to least in need of assistance.

Students read a teacher-written story about underprivileged people seeking shelter and summarize the main points.

Students watch a public service video and identify who needs help, where they are, how the organization helps, and how a similar American organization can learn from them.

Interpersonal Task: Students video-record themselves role-playing requesting and obtaining things in a hotel, in a homestay, and in a restaurant in a manner that reflects their cultural understanding of what and how one can obtain what one might need in these various Chinese contexts.

Presentational Task: Students reflect in the target language about the topic of "Wants and Needs," considering their own wants and needs as well as others' wants and needs. They may draw from needs they examined in the interpretive tasks and needs and wants they identified in the interpersonal task. This can be a story, a dialogue, a letter, or any format the students choose, and students can draw pictures to support meaning in their writing.

Example 2: Intermediate Low Level German Unit

Civil Courage

OVERVIEW: Students complete tasks that ask them to consider situations that they may encounter on a day-to-day basis and how they might respond in a way that advocates for those whose rights are being infringed upon.

Interpretive Tasks:

Students watch a short film, *Schwarzfahrer*, by Pepe Danquart and describe the actions taken or not taken by various individuals.

Students listen to the song *10 Arten von Zivilcourage* and identify main themes.

Students read an article from an online newspaper about how to engage in civil courage in different situations and create a graphic organizer to represent the main suggestions for each situation.

Interpersonal Task: Students are given several scenarios in which they discuss with a partner. How would they get involved? What might they say or do? Which actions may or may not be appropriate for each scenario?

Presentational Task: Students create either a graphic or a short video advocating for others to engage more in civil courage. They detail steps they can take to advocate for others who face injustice or danger or whose rights may be infringed upon.

Figure 3.4. Examples of IPAs for a novice-level Chinese class and an intermediate-level German class

Now it's your turn to develop a summative, authentic assessment for the unit. Develop a performance-based assessment using the IPA framework described above. (For more specific and detailed instructions on writing an IPA, see Adair-Hauck et al.'s (2013) *Implementing Integrated Performance Assessment.*)

Fill in the rectangles below with the context overview for your assessment and the integrated interpretive, interpersonal, and presentational tasks. As you work, refer back to the descriptions and the examples in Chinese and German.

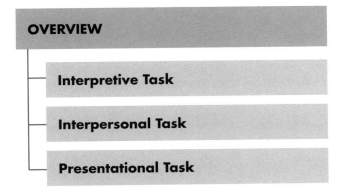

Teachers often ask about the best way to evaluate students or assign a grade when using an IPA. Using a rubric offers two advantages: (1) It enables you to evaluate students, or give them a grade, based on their performance. (2) More importantly, it helps you to express your expectations for the activity and provide very specific feedback on areas of strength and areas for further development. See Appendix F for examples of how social justice components can be incorporated into a rubric for an IPA. More specific instruction on creating rubrics for IPAs can be accessed in *The Keys to Planning for Learning* (Clementi & Terrill, 2017), *The Keys to Assessing Language Performance: A Teacher's Manual* (Sandrock, 2015), and *Implementing Integrated Performance Assessments* (Adair-Hauck et al., 2013).

Steps 4 and 5: Create Formative Assessments, Learning Activities, and Lesson Plans

The final steps in this process focus on designing activities that help students meet the learning objectives you have planned, and integrating them with formative assessments throughout so you can track and adapt your lessons based on students' learning and development levels. These steps will build off of the first three steps described above. We also encourage you to remain open to the idea that planning the lessons might lead you to change parts of your summative assessments, or even alter your initial objectives. This is likely to happen the first time you teach your original unit.

These steps will be explained in detail in Chapter 5. In that chapter, we will support you with steps to create individual lesson plans that connect back to your social justice understandings and the objectives you planned thus far in the process.

Putting It All Together

At this point you might put the ideas you worked through in this chapter into a complete unit plan. You are welcome to use our template, or a more detailed unit plan template such as the one available in *Keys to Planning* (Clementi & Terrill, 2017). (Appendix A has a list of themes, activity ideas, and online resources, and Appendix B has our suggested template.) To see how these steps fit together, examine the full unit plans found at the end of this chapter for the novice-level Chinese unit and the intermediate-level German unit. (See Appendix C for an additional example of a unit within the planning template we recommend.)

Conclusion

You might feel very confident about your unit plan ideas, or you might be feeling a little uneasy about them. Unit planning is complex, and sometimes even messy. Creating strong essential questions and goals that align with standards is very demanding, even for veteran teachers. Beyond the essential questions and goals, creating authentic, valid, reliable assessments is also challenging. This type of planning takes time, research, creativity, and patience. One of your best resources for this process is a colleague (or several colleagues) with whom to collaborate. Unit planning is definitely a place where a critical friend can push your thinking and help you think through challenges.

Discussion Questions

1. Revisit the vignette about Li and Elena. How would you articulate Li's social justice goals? How do the teachers in the vignette view the role of culture in their units? How does their viewpoint guide the way they plan to teach culture?

2. In Step 1, you identified the theme, essential question(s) and the takeaway understanding(s) you will address in your original unit. How did you identify this theme, the essential question(s), and the takeaway understanding (e.g., through personal experience, other texts, or Internet research)? What are other ways to identify themes and takeaway understandings that address social justice issues?

3. Look over the goals and standards that were unpacked in Step 2. What do you think are important considerations when identifying goals and standards to be met in a unit? How did the *World-Readiness Standards* overlap with the *Social Justice Standards*? Are there changes you would make to either of the unit plans to better align the goals, *World-Readiness Standards,* and *Social Justice Standards*?

4. Examine the two-unit plan examples closely. The unit plans in their entirety can be found below. What are strengths of each of the plans? What might you change about each of the plans? How might you adapt these themes to your own teaching context and/or to the proficiency levels of your students? What kinds of questions would you ask the teacher about each of the unit plans?

REFERENCES

Adair-Hauck, B., Glisan, E., & Troyan, F. (2013). *Implementing integrated performance assessment.* Alexandria, VA: American Council on the Teaching of Foreign Languages.

American Council on the Teaching of Foreign Languages (ACTFL). (2012, April 3). *Aligning the national standards for learning languages with the Common Core State Standards.* Retrieved from http://www.actfl.org/sites/default/files/pdfs/Aligning_CCSS_Language_Standards_v6.pdf

American Council on the Teaching of Foreign Languages (ACTFL). (2014). NCSSFL-ACTFL *Global can-do benchmarks.* Retrieved from http://www.actfl.org/sites/default/files/pdfs/Can-Do_Statements.pdf

Clementi, D., & Terrill, L. (2017). *Keys to planning for learning: Effective curriculum, unit and lesson design* (2nd Ed.) Alexandria, VA: American Council on the Teaching of Foreign Languages.

Curtain, H. & Dahlberg, C. (2016). *Languages and learners: Making the match* (5th Ed). New York, NY: Pearson Education, Inc.

Farrell, T. S. C. (2002). Lesson Planning. In Richards, J. C. & Renandya, W. A. (Eds.), *Methodology in language teaching: An anthology of current practice* (pp. 30-39). New York, NY: Cambridge University Press.

Glisan, E. W., Adair-Hauck, B., Koda, K., Sandrock, S. P., & Swender, E. (2003). *ACTFL integrated performance assessment.* Yonkers, NY: American Council on the Teaching of Foreign Languages.

Hall, J. K. (2001). *Methods for teaching foreign languages: Creating a community of learners in the classroom.* Columbus, OH: Prentice-Hall.

McTighe, J. & Wiggins, G. (2013). *Essential questions: Opening doors to student learning.* Alexandria, VA: Association for Supervision and Curriculum Development.

National Governors Association Center for Best Practices & Council of Chief State School Officers. (2010). *Common Core State Standards.* Washington, DC: National Governors Association Center for Best Practices, Council of Chief State School Officers.

National Standards Collaborative Board. (2015). *World-Readiness Standards for Learning Languages.* 4th ed. Alexandria, VA: Author.

New Jersey Department of Education. (2014). *Model Curriculum: World Languages.* Retrieved from http://www.state.nj.us/education/modelcurriculum/wl/

New Jersey Department of Education. (2014). *New Jersey Core Curriculum State Standards: World Languages.* Retrieved from: http://www.state.nj.us/education/cccs/2014/wl/

Sandrock, P. (2010). *The keys to assessing language performance.* Alexandria, VA: The American Council on the Teaching of Foreign Languages.

Shrum, J. & Glisan, E. W. (2016) *Teacher's handbook: Contextualized language instruction.* (5th Ed.) Boston, MA: Heinle.

TeachThought Staff. (2018). *A giant list of really good essential questions.* Retrieved from https://www.teachthought.com/pedagogy/examples-of-essential-questions/

Wiggins, G. & McTighe, J. (2005). *Understanding by design* (2nd ed.). Alexandria, VA: Assn. for Supervision & Curriculum Development.

Table 3.3. Novice High Level Chinese Unit Frame (Written by Reed Riggs)

Theme and Essential Question(s)

Needs and Wants: *What Do We Need Most and How Do We Get It?*

Social Justice Takeaway Understanding(s)

Although helping others in need is important, successful action takes place, not by being a "savior," but by empowering those in need through sustainable practices that support them to help each other.

Goals

- Students will be able to request and obtain things they need and want in hotels, homestays, and restaurants.
- Students will be able to identify the difference between needs and wants in their own daily lives and in the lives of others in both the U.S. and in China.
- Students will be able to describe one Chinese organization that helps Chinese people in need (where, who and how they help) and one US organization that helps American people in need.
- Students will be able to compare and contrast the role and type of help the Chinese and American organizations give.

World-Readiness Standards	Teaching Tolerance Social Justice Standards
Communication: - Interpersonal, Interpretive, Presentational **Cultures:** - Practices to Perspectives: Staying in a hotel or with a family in China; eating in Chinese restaurants; practices of domestic aid organizations - Products to Perspectives: Chinese hotels; Chinese homes; Chinese restaurants; products from domestic aid organizations **Connections:** - Making Connections: Social studies and understanding lives of people in China - Acquiring Information and Diverse Perspectives: - Text from domestic aid organizations in China **Comparisons:** - Language Comparisons: Use of reference words like this, that, here; there; descriptions using names, numbers, places - Cultural Comparisons: Comparisons of needs and wants in China versus U.S. in different contexts—in homes, in hotels, in restaurants; domestic aid organizations in U.S. versus China—Who is in need? What do they need? **Communities:** - School and Global Communities: Recognition and identification of needs and wants within their own school and communities - Lifelong Learning: Ability to understand typical practices when traveling in China	**Diversity:** - Students will develop language and knowledge to ac-curately and respectfully describe how people (including themselves) are both similar to and different from each other and others in their identity groups. **Justice:** - Students will recognize that power and privilege influence relationships on interpersonal, intergroup and institutional levels and consider how they have been affected by those dynamics.

Summative Assessments

Interpretive Communication
- Students examine infographics about groups in need and rank them from most to least in need of assistance.
- Students read a teacher-written story about underprivileged people seeking shelter and summarize the main points.
- Students watch a public service video and identify who needs help, where they are, how the organization helps, and how a similar American organization can learn from them.

Interpersonal Communication
- Students video-record themselves role-playing requesting and obtaining things in a hotel, a homestay and a restaurant in a manner that reflects their cultural understanding of what and how one can obtain what one might need in these various Chinese contexts.

Presentational Communication
- Students reflect in the target language on the topic of *Wants and Needs*, considering their own wants and needs as well as those of others. This can be a story, a dialogue, a letter, or any format the students choose. Students can draw pictures to support meaning in their writing.

Table 3.4. Intermediate Low Level German Unit Frame

Theme and Essential Question(s)

Civil Courage—How Can I Speak Out and Take Action?

Social Justice Takeaway Understanding(s)

- Civil courage can be enacted in big and small ways.
- Individuals can make a difference by advocating for the rights of others.
- A person's ability to carry out civil courage can vary based on their background and own experiences.

Goals

- Students will know that resistance movements throughout history have been carried out by citizens who have felt called to act against injustice.
- Students will be able to compare and contrast various acts of civil courage, both small and large.
- Students will be able to explain steps they can take toward action in certain situations.
- Students will be able to describe their own point of view and others' perspectives regarding injustices and action that may be necessary.

World-Readiness Standards

Communication:
- Interpersonal, Interpretive, Presentational

Cultures:
- Practices to Perspectives: Acts of civil courage among different groups of citizens.
- Products to Perspectives: Various authentic text put out by groups advocating for civil courage (leaflets, social media, videos, images).

Connections:
- Making Connections: Historical resistance movements such as Nazi resistance groups during WWII.
- Acquiring Information and Diverse Perspectives: Leaflets written by Nazi resistance groups and other authentic text; sites of resistance through virtual field trips.

Comparisons:
- Language Comparisons: Use of subjunctive in English and in German.
- Cultural Comparisons: Historical acts of resistance and civil courage in German and the U.S. (Nazi re-sistance, Civil Rights Movement) and more current acts of resistance and civil courage in both countries (Women's March; Me, Too; Anti-Nazi; Anti-Pegida—Patriotic Europeans Against the Islamisation of the West).

Communities:
- School and Global Communities: Ways in which students can engage in small acts of civil courage, both within and outside of their college community.

Teaching Tolerance Social Justice Standards

Justice:
- Students will recognize unfairness on the individual level (e.g., biased speech) and injustice at the institu-tional or systemic level (e.g., discrimination).
- Students will analyze the harmful impact of bias and injustice on the world, historically and today

Action:
- Students will express empathy when people are ex-cluded or mistreated because of their identities and concern when they themselves experience bias.
- Students will recognize their own responsibility to stand up to exclusion, prejudice and injustice.
- Students will speak up with courage and respect when they or someone else has been hurt or wronged by bi-as.
- Students will make principled decisions about when and how to take a stand against bias and injustice in their everyday lives and will do so despite negative peer or group pressure.

Summative Assessments

Interpretive Communication
- Students watch a short film, *Schwarzfahrer,* by Pepe Danquart and describe the actions taken or not taken by various individuals.
- Students listen to the song *10 Arten von Zivilcourage* and identify main themes.
- Students read an article from an online newspaper about how to engage in civil courage in different situa-tions and create a graphic organiz-er to represent the main suggestions for each situation.

Interpersonal Communication
- Students are given several scenarios to discuss with a partner. Should they get involved? Why or why not? How would they involve them-selves? What might they say or do? Which actions may or may not be ap-propriate for each scenario?

Presentational Communication
- Students create either a graphic or a short video advo-ating for others to engage more in civil courage and detailing steps they can take to advocate for others who face injustice or danger or whose rights may be infringed upon.

CHAPTER 4
Adapting Existing Curricula for Social Justice

In many K-16 educational institutions across the United States, the scope, sequence, activities, and assessments used in traditional world language programs come at least partially from a textbook series. This is not true for all classrooms, however, and teachers who use textbooks do not all use them in the same way. Immersion programs, which focus on teaching content, follow set core curricula, but the thematic units and types of materials immersion programs use can vary greatly among districts. Additionally, many teachers in more traditional language programs do not use a textbook series at all, but instead create instruction units based on a story or a thematic focus.

Regardless of whether the teacher has a more prescribed curriculum in place or has flexibility with the curriculum, and regardless of the teacher's approach to teaching language and culture, there are a variety of ways to adapt existing classroom curriculum to incorporate social justice understandings. In some cases this will entail an enhancement of what is already in the curricular materials and assessments, while in others it will involve a more elaborate process of creating a parallel curriculum. As in Chapter 3, we will provide examples from different curricula and contexts, and you will be able to practice using your own curriculum and ideas.

A Glimpse into the Classroom

Jordana and Thomas are Spanish professors at the same university. They both teach first year Spanish courses, so most of their students are at the novice proficiency level. In their first- and second-year courses they use a textbook. They try to stay on a similar schedule and are now on the third chapter of their textbook, which covers topics such as the home and family. Jordana and Thomas each take a different approach to teaching the material in Chapter 3: Jordana adapts the chapter to integrate more materials from outside of the textbook-provided supplements, while Thomas primarily uses the materials included with the textbook series and supplements them with a few of his own materials.

Knowing she must follow the textbook's scope and sequence to keep pace with Thomas, Jordana introduces students to a variety of families one would find in Spanish-speaking countries, using pictures and videos she has found on the Internet. These include images of a single parent family in Spain, a nuclear Afro-Peruvian family, an Argentinian family with extended family members living together, a Cuban family with a child with special needs, and a Mexican-American family with two mothers and their two children living in San Antonio, Texas. She uses these pictures not only to introduce the family vocabulary to students and activate prior knowledge of adjectives and the verb *tener* (to have), but also to engage students in a discussion of the different types of families that exist in Spanish-speaking countries. She also hopes to engage them with the idea that families may have different rights and privileges based on their compositions. Jordana also leads a discussion in English to help students understand what makes a family vary from one Spanish-speaking country to the next. Students are asked to compare and contrast these various views.

Thomas, again, focuses on textbook-provided materials. On the first day of the chapter, he asks the students to read a cultural blurb from the textbook about homes in Spain and shows a video from the text's ancillary materials depicting a teenager, Hugo, at home with his family. As students watch the video, they answer questions from the listening workbook page Thomas photocopied for them. Then he shows them a video his Dominican friend Yefri recorded of his home and family, stopping the video periodically to allow students to answer questions. After the videos, Thomas has students work in small groups to compare the two homes and families in the videos. Then he activates students' prior knowledge of adjectives and the verb *tener* by asking them to answer simple questions in small groups about their own homes and families. Finally, in English, he asks the students to discuss their homes in comparison with what they have now read and watched, letting students also ask questions they could not ask in the target language.

To think through these vignettes, please answer these questions:

1. How does each teacher incorporate culture related to families and the home into the unit?

2. Which teacher do you feel has an approach that is more informed by social justice education? Why do you feel that way?

3. How could the teachers adapt their lessons more to teach for social justice?

4. What are some strengths and weaknesses of each teacher's approach to introducing the unit to the students? What would you do to address the weaknesses if you were the teacher in each case?

Approaching World Language Curriculum with an Eye to Social Justice Issues

In this section, we discuss various approaches to teaching languages with examples of what an integration of social justice might look like in each approach. You will find sections on adapting textbook curricula, comprehensible input-focused curricula, immersion curricula, other content-based curricula, service-learning curricula, and project-based curricula, followed by steps you can take to adapt your curriculum, regardless of the types of materials you use in your classes. Along the way will be opportunities for you to work with your own curriculum.

Adapting Textbook Curricula

Textbooks tend not to include references to social justice issues or more critical aspects of culture. Although many textbook companies have taken strides to integrate culture and context and may mention the standards, relying heavily on the textbook does not guarantee that instruction is informed by second language acquisition (SLA) theory or that SLA theory and standards are the driving force behind the materials (Shrum & Glisan, 2016). Shrum and Glisan (2016) also argue that teachers must adapt textbooks to include real-world contexts, links to other

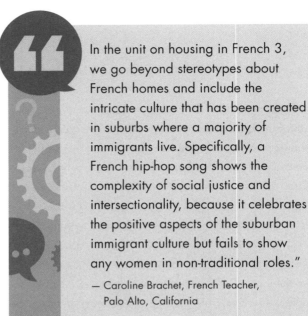

In the unit on housing in French 3, we go beyond stereotypes about French homes and include the intricate culture that has been created in suburbs where a majority of immigrants live. Specifically, a French hip-hop song shows the complexity of social justice and intersectionality, because it celebrates the positive aspects of the suburban immigrant culture but fails to show any women in non-traditional roles."

— Caroline Brachet, French Teacher, Palo Alto, California

disciplines, and opportunities to value students' varied identities and varied perspectives, ideas, and answers. They underscore the importance of "personalizing the exercises to the lives of the students" and moving beyond just "one correct answer" (p. 61).

Wiggins & McTighe (2006) caution that textbooks are rarely designed to promote critical thinking and inquiry of more complex, thought-provoking topics in its subject. As authors of world language textbooks ourselves, we understand some of these limitations. Yet we also suggest that you can help students progress beyond the textbook's information while still meeting state, district and curricular expectations about what will be taught in your classes. That is, you can still follow the **scope and sequence** while incorporating unique, engaging social justice activities into your classes.

The textbook chapter's cultural sections, sometimes called **cultural blurbs,** often serve multiple purposes as one strives to integrate social justice topics into the chapter. If you completely adapt the chapter by giving it a new overarching theme with clear social justice entry points, these blurbs can inspire teachers to conceptualize a new theme for the unit. If the chapter is about education, for example, and one target culture contains a blurb about the cost of attending university, this could bring about questions of access and ability to compare and contrast with access to education in the U.S. This chapter could be reconceptualized with the theme of "Equity and Access to Education."

By reconceptualizing the chapter under a new theme, education can be regarded from a number of perspectives. In a country with a high number of immigrants and refugees, how many of these students attend the highest tier of secondary school? How many attend post-secondary institutions? Why do students have fewer academic opportunities in some countries? What kinds of access to resources do students typically have? In what way does this access vary? Which students are most likely to have access to strong educational opportunities? In essence, a reconceptualization of the chapter under a new theme based on the chapter's cultural blurbs can open it up to many avenues of exploring social justice topics.

However, if a reconceptualization of the entire chapter seems unfeasible, simply use the cultural blurbs as entry points to an examination of social justice topics. Although cultural blurbs often contain interesting information that fits well with the topic of the chapter, they tend to take a one-sided view of the culture, sometimes reinforcing stereotypes. It is vital to problematize these one-sided perspectives. In the planning process, closely examining these cultural blurbs can let you see how social justice themes may fit as jumping off-points for exploring the blurb's topic more deeply.

For example, in one textbook we examined, a cultural blurb describes well-known families who own businesses in Germany. However, closer examination reveals that the represented families are upper class and make millions of dollars yearly from their businesses; this can be problematized. In many countries, family-owned businesses make significant contributions to their communities, providing not only for their families, but also providing gathering spaces and places of belonging. For instance, in Germany, Turkish-German family-owned businesses not only contribute to the German culture in significant ways, but also preserve traditions, the Turkish language, and a sense of belonging among those who claim Turkish-German heritage. Students can examine these types of small-scale family-owned businesses and compare and contrast them

to family-owned businesses in their own communities. Questions students could consider about family-owned businesses, both within their own cultures and in the target cultures, may include:

- How do these businesses affect the families who own them and the surrounding community?

- How can we support and/or encourage these families and their businesses?

- If immigrants or refugees own the businesses, how are they received in the surrounding community? What kind of value do these family-owned businesses bring to the communities and to the groups of immigrants and refugees?

Vocabulary lists found in textbooks may also contain one-sided perspectives of the target culture(s), but the words themselves deserve further examination, problematization and discussion. Regarding gendered vocabulary, it may be necessary to provide students with additional vocabulary that represents non-binary people so the students can accurately talk about themselves and others.

Additionally, some gendered vocabulary requires more careful examination. For example, the word for "doctor" in French, *médecin,* is inherently male; there is no female version, although one is able to use *médecin* to describe female doctors. Students can be asked to consider why they think that may be and what kinds of values that aspect of the word, itself, might impart. The types of vocabulary words used in the list may also contain underlying values that do not accurately represent the values, beliefs and day-to-day lives of people who live in the target culture(s).

A list of family members may not allow students to accurately describe the compositions of their own families, nor may it represent the variety of families found in target culture(s). A list of items in a home may be skewed toward upper-middle-class families, a socioeconomic status neither all students nor all members of the target culture(s) can claim. A list of careers may be more representative of white-collar jobs, even though many find success in blue-collar positions, and many target culture(s) place a high value on blue-collar jobs.

The chapter's topic itself may also serve as an entry point for social justice topics. A typical topic in a Latin textbook chapter focuses on the lives of Romans of various social classes. One topic often explored is the treatment of slaves and their role in Roman society. Whitney Hellenbrand and Elissabeth Legendre, Latin teachers in Chicago, adapted this chapter from their level-one textbook, *Cambridge Latin Course*. The unit goals included the ability to describe how class status and colonization affected Romans' lives from different perspectives. They also wanted students to reflect on the oppressed voices that are missing in ancient texts that have survived to the modern age. This unit also provided an opportunity to meet the Making Connections Standard, drawing on social studies and English Language Arts content. Students read *Frederick Douglass: The Last Day of Slavery* and Horace's *Ode 1.38* and were asked to compare and contrast the lives of Roman slaves and American slaves. This deepened their knowledge of both Roman and American history and developed their ability to analyze literature. (See Appendix E for Hellenbrand's and Legendre's unit overview.)

Teachers need not feel too hemmed in by a textbook's scope and sequence. There are a number of ways, both big and small, to integrate topics of social justice to enrich the textbook chapter and its ancillary materials.

Adapting Comprehensible Input-focused Curricula

Teachers who self-identify as teaching with **Comprehensible Input (CI)** strategies can vary widely in their instructional practices. There is not one way to easily characterize a CI curriculum, although the goal is always language acquisition through comprehensible input into the language. In this section we will address three common components often used within a CI-focused classroom: (1) incorporating new vocabulary and structures (sometimes called target structures); (2) storytelling and story-asking; and (3) reading, usually in the form of free voluntary reading or reading novels. (There are multiple perspectives within the CI-teaching community on virtually all of these instructional strategies, and we will not explore these issues in depth here. If a reader is interested in a general introduction to these concepts, we offer some recommendations at the end of the chapter.)

In a CI-focused curriculum, the selection and repetition of **newly-introduced vocabulary, words, and phrases,** also called "language chunks" (Bex, 2015), can take many forms. There are many ways to focus instruction on these language chunks, including but not limited to personalized questions and answers (PQA), MovieTalks (Hastings, 2012) and PictureTalks, and Total Physical Response (TPR) techniques. Sheltering instruction around new language chunks should represent and validate all students in the classroom. Pictures and videos that provide a path to the language chunks should represent a variety of ethnicities, socioeconomic backgrounds, different physical abilities, and gender representations. Teachers should avoid only focusing on rich celebrities, athletes, or politicians to illustrate points, instead also privileging the students' home cultures and identities.

Additionally, doing MovieTalks with films in the target language can touch on social justice themes in depth, bringing in topics that extend beyond the language chunks but provide comprehensible input. PQA should allow all students to contribute in an accepting environment and should allow for an exchange of information about what students wish to share about their lives. Finally, use of TPR techniques should account for disabilities students might have in the classroom with making gestures or moving around.

Story-Telling and Story-Asking, common practices in CI-focused classrooms, offer key opportunities to teach for social justice. To begin, teachers must question their assumptions about the universality of certain stories they might tell. For instance, a story about shopping in a store, even if using fictional characters or celebrities students suggest in the class, might affect students differently if they have recently been accused of shoplifting, or if they consistently struggle to get shopping money. As with focused instruction on language chunks, teachers must be aware that representations matter, and that characters in stories should represent a variety of backgrounds, not limited to celebrities, politicians and athletes. Stories that revolve around love stories should allow for different gender pairings when possible. Families in the stories should include non-traditional family structures. Adjectives used to describe people should include options beyond physical appearances and relate to the target culture(s) (e.g., optimistic, hard-working). Teachers are not obligated to take every suggestion from students, and pushing them to move in a more representative direction can lead to a more equitable classroom.

Additionally, the stories can include social justice-focused issues, e.g., inequality, discrimination, access to resources, advocacy, and local, regional, national and international conflicts. Though students must be kept engaged with comprehensible stories, interesting, engaging stories about these topics can be considered in several ways, including:

- stories about resolving local injustices or debates, with unexpected results;

- stories about famous activists or trailblazers from the target culture meeting one another outside of their regular timelines;

- stories in which underrepresented or minoritized groups in the target culture play pivotal roles.

Every single story need not be transformed in this way, but CI-focused teachers can continue to expand their repertoires of stories to incorporate more social justice issues.

Reading. This usually includes free voluntary reading or reading novels. This area is perhaps the easiest to adapt to social justice education, because it involves finding and using classroom materials that address social justice topics while also incorporating focal language chunks. Spanish and French teachers can select from a wide variety of sheltered-language readers intended for CI-focused classrooms, many of which address such issues as discrimination and oppression (see list at end of chapter). Other novels might not explicitly have these same themes, but through the development of a directed class discussion teachers can relate many texts to themes such as identity, disability, difference, isolation, bullying, and acceptance. As readers develop higher levels of proficiency, short stories and articles about events in the target culture(s) can expose them to key concepts in social justice education. Teachers of other languages, who may not have as many sheltered-language readers available to them, can create or find shorter readings that include the language chunks targeted in the class context at that time.

Ultimately, CI-focused instruction, with its focus on developing language proficiency through extensive input, has many pathways to integrating topics of social justice education. With some thought and preparation, like teachers using any other approach, CI-focused teachers can successfully incorporate social justice themes in their curricula. Activities and assessments that emphasize the interpretation of comprehensible texts can be found throughout this chapter and the rest of the book, so teachers who self-identify as CI teachers can build on those samples for inspiration.

Adapting K-12 Immersion Curricula

In immersion programs, at least 50% of subject (content) matter instruction at the elementary level occurs through the foreign/second/minority language for a minimum of six years. At the secondary level, at least two subject matter courses are taught in the foreign/second/minority language (Fortune & Tedick, 2008). The goals of immersion programs are academic achievement at or above grade level, additive bilingualism/biliteracy, and the development of cultural or multicultural competence (Tedick & Wesely, 2015). The percentage of instruction given in the foreign/second/minority language might vary across contexts, depending on the linguistic background of the students in the program, the sociolinguistic environment surrounding the schools, and the program's purpose. However, given that mastery of academic content is essential in immersion settings, all immersion teachers must teach the district's curriculum in all content areas (e.g., science, math, social studies).

As such, our primary recommendations for integrating social justice education into immersion programs focus on **finding entry points for introducing social justice topics within the content area curriculum.** This process might resemble that for adapting textbooks: examine the scope and sequence, identify where culture comes into the curriculum, and look at vocabulary lists. Additionally, immersion teachers should consult the content-specific standards and guidelines that frame their work. For instance, if a sixth-grade two-way immersion (bilingual) science class is required to address standards related to environment and climate, the teacher can guide the students through connecting more with social justice issues involving conservation in different cultures.

Immersion teachers should also **consult the work done in social justice education in those content areas** as they focus on the connections with language or culture education. Many different content areas have strong histories of social justice education. Immersion teachers can benefit from familiarizing themselves with and building on the traditions and practices in the specific content areas. General resources about social justice education— e.g., the Teaching Tolerance website—can offer starting points in identifying appropriate teaching resources.

Finally, immersion programs present unique possibilities for **developing interdisciplinary projects** that address social justice issues. One such example is a unit developed for third-grade immersion and used with third-grade Chinese immersion students at XinXing Academy in Hopkins, Minnesota. This unit, called *Engineering is Elementary® Just Passing Through: Designing Model Membranes,* allows students to develop their knowledge and skills in Chinese language arts, science and engineering, math, and social studies and culture (Fortune, Wieland, & MMIC Team, 2012). In the unit, the teachers address the following essential questions, all of which have entry points for social justice topics: "How can observing nature help us solve problems? How can we learn from our mistakes? What is a bioengineer? How and why are countries the same or different? How do humans impact the environment?" Students examine scarcity of resources and resource conservation, comparing and contrasting cultural products, practices, and perspectives in El Salvador, the U.S., and China. They also examine their own roles within their communities to work for environmental justice. An additional entry point for social justice in this unit can be to highlight the role of women and underrepresented minorities in science and engineering (Fortune, Wieland, & MMIC Team, 2012; see link to entire unit in reference list).

Integrating social justice education with immersion education can offer an important new possibility for the idea of teaching content through language. In the next section, we will look at another type of content-focused instruction.

Adapting K-16 Content-Driven Curricula

When we think about **content-driven curricula** or **content-based instruction** (CBI), we tend to think primarily about immersion programs. Certainly, on the continuum of language-driven to content-driven, immersion programs fit squarely in a focus on content, which Met (1999) defined as "cognitively demanding and engaging… material that extends beyond the target language or target culture" (p. 150). CBI does take place in programs other than immersion, sometimes at the K-12 level as elementary (FLES), middle-school and high-school teachers seek to create cognitively demanding units that align with the academic curriculum in place at that grade level. However, we see CBI take place often at the post-secondary level in upper division language courses in particular. For instance, course offerings will include such topics as art and architecture, business, politics, Spanish for medical use, literature, and history.

It is common for content-driven courses, such as upper division college-level language coursework, to rely on authentic resources.

One starting point for integrating social justice into existing units is to examine the literature and other materials used in the course. Literature courses tend to introduce students to the "classics" and the literary canon. This has benefits and drawbacks, but Chiariello (2017) suggests "remixing the classics list" (p. 29), offering a number of strategies for making literature more inclusive, which will provide more entry points for you to integrate social justice topics:

1. Ask yourself how the literature meets the objectives of the course and if any other materials could be added that would still meet the objectives.

2. Ask students to read the texts, classics included, through multiple lenses. The Latin unit in Appendix E focused on the reading of *Metamorphoses* is a good example of using a classic but problematizing themes that arise, such as gender roles, to examine the topic through the lenses of different characters.

3. Teach students to think critically about whose voices are represented and whose are missing in the text.

4. Use more excerpts, rather than full texts, to give students a wider variety of readings on a particular topic.

5. Link the literature to current events. In the world language classroom, this may mean linking readings to events taking place in the U.S. or in a target culture.

Another content-driven example is a unit developed by Tália González focused on Latino civil rights, a cognitively demanding unit that draws on academic content from social studies and English language arts that is grade-level-appropriate for the students. González aims for students to understand that the challenges marginalized groups face are structural and that a number of courageous Latino leaders have worked to dismantle those structures. Students read and analyze text written by Latinos (language arts), learn about such important cases as Méndez v. Westminster (social studies), discuss an image of "separate is never equal" (social studies), listen to an interview with Sylvia Méndez (social studies), and draft formal letters to politicians (language arts). Though this unit was developed for eighth graders, it can be adapted to older students in high school and college by using readings and other materials developmentally and academically appropriate for the students' levels. González also gives her students a presentational task of teaching an important civil rights case to third graders. While this is appropriate for eighth graders, swapping this out for a more cognitively demanding presentational task, such as a formal research paper, may be more appropriate for the post-secondary level.

Content-driven units lend themselves nicely to integration of social justice topics, sometimes without changing the content at all, but simply by problematizing it, viewing it through different lenses, and asking students to question and think critically about the content covered.

Adapting Service-Learning Curricula

Service learning is "a research-based teaching method where guided or classroom learning is applied through action that addresses an authentic community need in a process that allows for youth initiative and provides struc-tured time for reflection on the service experience and demonstration of acquired skills and knowledge" (Kaye, 2010, p. 9). Above all, service learning connects classroom content to community needs. Service learning in world language contexts often comprises such projects as providing translating services, helping communities in need in other areas of the world, and advocating for the needs of individuals or communities where the target language is spoken. Service learning need not meet social justice objectives to be considered service learning, and it does not do so automatically (Einfeld & Collins, 2008). Service learning opportunities can take a variety of forms; some can focus students on individuals rather than systemic or pervasive issues of social justice. These are not necessarily poor service learning opportunities, but they may not have been structured to encourage social justice learning.

On the other hand, social justice education is often very closely linked with action, often intended to encourage students to take action to address inequalities and solve problems outside of the classroom framework (Nieto, 2010). However, service learning offers useful guidelines for those interested in pursuing more action-oriented social justice projects with students.

We suggest taking these steps to connect service-learning opportunities with your social justice activities and projects:

1. *Collaborate to establish shared social justice objectives* with the community organizations you work with.

2. *Identify and build on students' experiences and backgrounds* so they can better apply their skills and build on their prior knowledge. This is a central tenet of both service learning and social justice education. You can do this by allowing them to explore their preconceptions before the service learning begins and supporting them to revisit their personal reactions throughout the project.

3. *Provide space and time for reflection,* not just on individual experiences, but also on more systemic issues those individual experiences suggest (Einfeld & Collins, 2008). Foster opportunities for students to examine any

deficit views related to the community or people being served. For instance, have your students contextualize an activity such as translating at a food bank, with an explicit discussion about why community members rely on the food bank's services.

4. *Plan for continuity and time investment* so students can truly understand the community they serve and the issues that community faces. Support students as they work toward developing empathy for others and relationships with individuals in the community.

Following these different recommendations can help your service-learning project also bring students closer to teaching for social justice.

Adapting Project-Based Learning Curricula

Project-based learning (PBL) engages students over a long period of time in student-centered, collaborative work on one unified project that seeks to answer a set of complex questions. The *Framework for High Quality Project-Based Learning* (HQPBL; 2018) identifies six criteria for strong PBL:

1. *Intellectual challenge and accomplishment*: students learn deeply, think critically, and strive for excellence.

2. *Authenticity*: Students work on projects that are meaningful and relevant to their culture, lives and future.

3. *Public product*: Students' work is publicly displayed, discussed, and critiqued.

4. *Collaboration*: Students collaborate in person or online and/or receive guidance from adult mentors and experts.

5. *Project management*: Students use a project management process by which they proceed effectively from project initiation to completion.

6. *Reflection*: Students reflect on their work and learning throughout the project.

In world language classrooms, PBL enables students to "engage in real life communication, in context, with real people, and across the globe" (Doehla, 2011).

To adapt PBL curricula to integrate social justice education, the most crucial decision is selecting a project that authentically addresses a social justice issue. In addition, the project should result in a public product that involves substantive action, not just reporting. Often this will take the form of advocacy or education for the public on the issue, designed to go beyond explaining a school project and instead engaging with promoting change in behavior or attitude about the issue.

In planning, teachers will need to pair the social justice issue with an appropriate activity that can be completed collaboratively and fulfill the other PBL requirements. For instance, students could investigate how many local municipal materials (about issues like weather alerts, utilities, and elections) are available to members of the target culture in their language and accessible to them. In working groups, the students can compile information about what is and is not available in the target language, and then interview target community members to see what other information they would want translated and how they would want it communicated to them (e.g., digitally, through mailings, or through posted flyers). Then the students can prepare a presentation for the local government about the target community's needs and even offer to provide some translations. They can reflect on their project experience throughout and after their project.

In social justice-focused PBL, students can collectively research, explore, and advocate about important social justice issues. They can address a complex question, working collaboratively, in a real-life context, and they can move the project to action using the public product as a forum to advocate for change.

Steps to Adapting Existing Units

Step 1: Identify the Point of Entry, Essential Questions, and Takeaway Understandings.
You will identify a point of entry in your curriculum where you can address social justice takeaway understandings, and then identify those understandings (Fig. 4.1). This will prepare you to write unit goals in the subsequent steps of this process.

In Chapter 1, we argued that almost every aspect of teaching world languages has social justice implications. World language curricula, be they textbook-based, CBI, and even CI materials, are full of entry points for social justice to be added to the unit and accompanying lessons. To begin, we recommend you look specifically for cultural elements and academic content topics open to social justice topic integration. If your existing unit, for example, has explicit connections to products, practices and perspectives, they can also be strong points of entry. Recall how social justice issues can be organized around products (focusing on access to and relationships with tangible and intangible resources), practices (arising from how people interact), and perspectives (stemming from attitudes and values).

For instance, science content lessons in an immersion context about the environment might lend themselves to social justice issues related to environmental justice (practices) and action in the form of a project students can lead in their own communities. Lessons about cuisine (common for more advanced novice-level learners) can address access to healthy foods or government-subsidized meals in schools (products). Lessons about media and mass communication in an upper division content-driven post-secondary language course can enable you to interrogate stereotypes and rhetoric related to different groups (perspectives). (For additional ideas, Appendix A lists various social justice understandings and related themes.)

As you scour your curriculum to find entry points, use these questions to help pinpoint ways to incorporate social justice understandings:

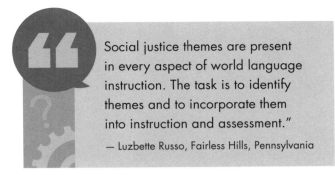

Social justice themes are present in every aspect of world language instruction. The task is to identify themes and to incorporate them into instruction and assessment."

— Luzbette Russo, Fairless Hills, Pennsylvania

- Is there a *history behind this cultural or academic topic* that might reveal past or present inequities?

- Are there *accepted truths* about this topic that can be challenged?

- Is this a topic that *people from different groups* (of socio-economic status/class, ethnicity, immigration status, abilities) might view differently?

Once you have identified a strong cultural topic or other content to serve as an entry point, identify a social justice takeaway understanding that fits. To determine this, ask yourself: "What are some of the important understandings related to social justice that I want students to be able to take with them as they continue their study of this language and culture?" At this point, consider collaborating with other educators in your school community, such as teachers of English language arts/literacy, mathematics, social studies/history, science, health, technology, or the arts, to engage your shared students in interdisciplinary learning around a social justice understanding. Such interdisciplinary planning fosters even deeper understanding and critical thinking for students. If you teach in an immersion program, we encourage you to collaborate with

Identify point of entry   Connect with standards   Identify the social justice **takeaway**

Figure 4.1. Overview of Step 1

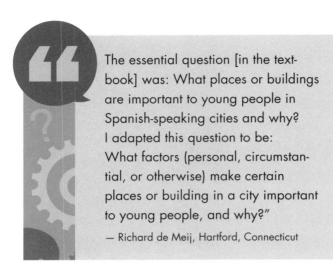

> "The essential question [in the textbook] was: What places or buildings are important to young people in Spanish-speaking cities and why? I adapted this question to be: What factors (personal, circumstantial, or otherwise) make certain places or building in a city important to young people, and why?"
>
> — Richard de Meij, Hartford, Connecticut

your grade-level colleagues on a thematic unit in which you can integrate social justice understandings.

As you seek an entry point, you may also consider whether you may be able to lead your students in taking action at some point in the unit. For example, Stephanie Owen-Lyons from Minneapolis found an entry point in a textbook chapter on food and eating to educate her high-school students on the inequities of wages and treatment of Latino(a) employees in tortilla factories. She led her students in an activity of writing letters to the transnational corporation in support of the employees' rights, allowing students to develop an understanding of a social justice topic while simultaneously working on their language skills. In the content-focused Spanish unit we introduce in this chapter, González tasks her eighth graders with writing letters in Spanish to politicians to share their concerns and perspectives about an important issue facing Latinos in the U.S.

In both of these examples, the teachers give students the tools for taking action. If it is not feasible to lead students in a form of action during the unit, consider still how you will put steps in place for them to know *how* to engage in action and have the agency to do so. This step, as we discussed in Chapter 1 with Hackman's (2005) framework, is key in teaching for social justice.

Step 2: Unpack Standards and Identify Unit Goals

You will identify how students will meet the World-Readiness, other content standards (if appropriate), and Social

Justice Standards. You will also list the unit goals students will be able to meet when they complete your adapted lessons. However, if you use a textbook, the textbook series may have already provided your language goals. In most cases, the textbook authors have already indicated what students will know and be able to do with the language. Some textbooks introduce them as communicative functions. Therefore, if you use these goals, your primary task will be to identify social justice goals that both connect with the language goals and build on them. Ask yourself the following as you complete this step:

- What should students know, and how will they make sense of *topics of social justice* in this unit?

- Is there any *overlap* between these social justice and the textbook-provided language goals? Can they be articulated *jointly?*

Two examples are below. The first, an example of Steps 1 and 2, is derived from a Level 2 French textbook, *Bon Voyage!* (Schmitt & Brillié Lutz, 2007) (see Table 4.1); the second comes from Spanish teacher Tália González, who developed a content-based unit for her eighth graders (see Table 4.2). As noted earlier, González's unit can be easily adapted to high-school and post-secondary students at the intermediate level.

In the first example, students explore the topic of healthy lifestyles from a variety of perspectives, gaining an understanding of how access and socioeconomic status affect one's ability to maintain a healthy lifestyle. The entry point into this unit came from examples of healthy practices depicted in the textbook chapter. These practices could be problematized and viewed in different ways.

In the second example, González found an entry point to examine Latinos' fight for civil rights through a previous unit on immigration and an oral history project. González wanted to enable her students to examine experiences in the U.S. through the lens of Dreamers and other Latinos who had demonstrated the agency to fight for their own rights and the civil rights of Latinos, in general. (Note: In both examples, we show the World-Readiness Standards (The National Standards Collaborative Board, 2015) and

Table 4.1. Novice High Level French Unit Adapted from the Level 2 Textbook *Bon Voyage!* (Schmitt & Brillié Lutz, 2007)

Point of Entry and Essential Question(s)

Chapter on Healthy Lifestyles — *How can culture and access impact one's health both positively and negatively? How I can support myself and others in maintaining a healthy lifestyle?*

Social Justice Takeaway Understanding(s)

- There are numerous views of a healthy lifestyle in the francophone world.
- The ability to maintain a healthy lifestyle depends on access (to healthcare, clean water, fresh food, etc.) and socioeconomic status.
- Empowerment of individuals in their own communities can lead to sustainable sources of fresh foods and income.

Goals

- Students will be able to describe their own and others' efforts to maintain a healthy lifestyle in four francophone countries (France, Canada, Senegal, Haiti) using vocabulary and reflexive verbs.
- Students will be able to explain how access to resources and socioeconomic status affect the health and lifestyles of people in the four francophone countries.
- Students will be able to compare and contrast access to resources in these four countries to access to resources in their own communities and cultures.
- Students will be able to identify the way Heifer International and other organizations support communities in need with sustainable practices that lead to agency among the community members.
- Students will be able to create a Heifer International campaign (in the target language) for their school to buy resources for a francophone community in need.

World-Readiness Standards

Communication:
- Interpersonal, Interpretive, Presentational

Cultures:
- Practices to Perspectives: Understanding the ways in which different people in different cultures participate in trying to maintain their health
- Products to Perspectives: Examination of resources available in students' own culture and in target cul-tures

Connections:
- Making Connections: Link to what students have learned previously in health classes
- Acquiring Information and Diverse Perspectives: Authentic videos that show how people live in the four francophone countries being explored

Comparisons:
- Language Comparisons: Reflexive verbs in French and English
- Cultural Comparisons: Comparisons of health practices and daily lives of people in the U.S. and in francophone countries

Communities:
- School and Global Communities: Schoolwide Heifer International campaign
- Lifelong Learning: Understanding the difference be-tween donation and empowering others in communities in need

Teaching Tolerance Social Justice Standards

Diversity:
- Students will develop language and knowledge to accurately and respectfully describe how people (including themselves) are both similar to and different from each other and others in their identity groups.

Justice:
- Students will recognize that power and privilege influence relationships on interpersonal, intergroup and institutional levels and will consider how they themselves have been affected by those dynamics.

Table 4.2. Intermediate Low Level Spanish Content-Based Instruction Unit (Written by Talía González)

Point of Entry and Essential Question(s)

Unit on Childhood – Latino Civil Rights – *What are civil rights? Who were important Latino civil rights leaders, and what kind of impact did they have? What are some modern civil rights issues that are important to Latinos? How have Latinos in the U.S. contributed to the fight for civil rights?*

Social Justice Takeaway Understanding(s)

- The challenges faced by oppressed groups are structural in nature.
- Both the oppressed and the privileged have the ability to effect change for oppressed groups and individuals.

Goals

- Students will be able to discuss what it means to be bicultural and/or bilingual, along with its benefits and challenges.
- Students will be able to present information on important Latino leaders and what they did to effect change.
- Students will be able to analyze the challenges Latinos face and discuss the need for powerful leaders to face these challenges.
- Students will be able to comprehend how the Latino experience has changed over time.
- Students will be able to describe important events that affect Latinos today.
- Students will be able to analyze literature born out of the U.S. Latino experience.

World-Readiness Standards	Teaching Tolerance Social Justice Standards
Communication: - Interpersonal, Interpretive, Presentational **Cultures:** - Practices to Perspectives: Latinos' acts to affect change and their beliefs - Products to Perspectives: Literature and other artifacts that represent Latinos' experiences in the U.S. **Connections:** - Making Connections: Social Studies—draw on what students are learning about civil rights in the U.S.; English Language Arts—analysis of literature and formal letter writing - Acquiring Information and Diverse Perspectives: Literature and other text written by Latinos in and outside of the U.S. **Comparisons:** - Language Comparisons: Grammatical concepts such as comparatives and direct and indirect object pronouns; vocabulary related to professions - Cultural Comparisons: Comparing and contrasting their own childhood and education experiences with those of immigrant Latinos **Communities:** - School and Global Communities: Invite guest speakers who are dreamers to form a panel - Lifelong Learning: Development of empathy and understanding of Latinos' experiences	**Identity:** - Students will develop language and historical and cultural knowledge that affirm and accurately describe their membership in multiple identity groups. - Students will recognize that people's multiple identities interact and create unique and complex individuals. **Diversity:** - Students will develop language and knowledge to accurately and respectfully describe how people (including themselves) are both similar to and different from each other and others in their identity groups. **Justice:** - Students will recognize that power and privilege influence relationships on interpersonal, intergroup and institutional levels and consider how they have been affected by those dynamics. - Students will identify figures, groups, events and a variety of strategies and philosophies relevant to the history of social justice around the world **Action:** - Students will speak up with courage and respect when they or someone else has been hurt or wronged by bias.

the Teaching Tolerance Social Justice Standards (2016), but when you complete this on your own, you can include your state standards and content standards.)

Your Turn!

Now it's your turn to adapt a unit from your own curriculum. You will identify the point of entry in the curricular materials, the essential question(s), and the social justice takeaway understanding(s). Then unpacking your unit goals, remembering that these merge social justice content, language, and cultural content. Finally, identify how you will meet the World-Readiness Standards and Teaching Tolerance Social Justice Standards, along with other appropriate or necessary standards.

Point of Entry and Essential Question(s)
Social Justice Takeaway Understanding(s)
Goals
World Readiness Standards
Communication: • Interpersonal, Interpretive, Presentational
Teaching Tolerance Social Justice Standards
Other Standards (optional)

Step 3: Create and Modify Assessments

You will want to use a variety of assessments that will check students' knowledge and skills, both formally and informally, while allowing you the opportunity to provide feedback and reflect on the students' progress. If you are working from a published textbook, it may be that you are using or modifying **publisher-supplied assessments.** Otherwise, you should examine assessments you currently use, because these can be modified to assess students' knowledge of the social justice content you are integrating into an existing unit. You can modify any types of assessments you give, be they more traditional or more authentic in nature. We also urge you to ensure that at least some of the summative and formative assessments focusing on your social justice unit are authentic in nature and assess students in multiple modes of communication. The extent to which you can do this will depend on a variety of factors: your program requirements and schedule, departmental and school support, etc.

We will begin with an explanation of some techniques you can use to modify the summative and formative assessments in your curriculum to better reflect a social justice approach. In this chapter, however, we will focus on adapting summative assessments. Formative assessments will be discussed in Chapter 5, but the techniques we explore in this chapter can be easily applied to any assessment. Finally, we offer examples of authentic summative assessments that fit with the social justice units illustrated above. (Consult Appendix F for rubrics that can be used to assess social justice summative assessments.)

Step 3, Part 1: Altering or Extending Existing Assessments

It is difficult to generalize about existing assessments in world language curriculum. Some may already include references to social justice issues, or may be open-ended enough to allow students to explore or reflect on social justice. Others may be more focused on mastery of discrete grammar or vocabulary concepts, thus may be harder to change. However, there are several paths to adding an assessment of social justice.

First, revisit the social justice takeaway understandings and unit goals you added in Steps 1 and 2. Recall that you are trying to identify evidence that the students have met these goals. Then we recommend one of the two following approaches to modifying existing materials:

1. Alter the context or background material of the assessment items.

2. Extend the assessment to add a social justice component.

Ask yourself the following as you complete this step:

- What is the most important thing to *retain* about the existing assessments?

- What is the most important thing to include in order to provide evidence that the *social justice takeaway understandings* can be met?

- Which approach is best, given your answer to the previous two questions: *to alter or to extend* the assessments?

When we focus on formative assessments in Chapter 5, you will need to verify that the changes you made to the summative assessments (e.g., tests and quizzes) are parallel to those you will make to the formative assessments (e.g., practice essays, worksheets, graded listening exercises). Below are examples of typical assessment activities in world language classes. (Note: Even traditional assessments can be altered or extended to incorporate social justice understandings.)

Examine some of the summative assessment tasks you ask students to complete, be they traditional or authentic in nature. Pick three assessment activities to modify, and fill out the table below.

Assessment	Type of Modification	Description

Step 3, Part 2: Replacing Existing Assessments
As discussed in Chapter 3, an authentic assessment allows students to engage in tasks that are contextualized

and may resemble a task they could complete in real life outside of the classroom. In this section, we provide some ideas to help you develop an Integrated Performance Assessment based on your curriculum. The IPA connects multiple tasks and allows teachers to assess students' ability to communicate in three modes: interpretive, interpersonal, and presentational. However, unlike Chapter 3, in which you created an original unit and based the IPA on your original ideas, this IPA will correspond to your existing curriculum.

1. Examine language and cultural themes: Map out the main language goals and cultural themes covered in the unit for which you are creating the IPA. As you examine your curriculum, concentrate on the language and themes and look for areas where they intersect. A graphic organizer can aid in this as well. This overlap is a good place to start building the IPA.

2. Establish a context: Based on the overlap between language goals and cultural themes, develop an overview for the IPA that incorporates both and allows for social justice understandings. For example, in the French unit described earlier, the textbook chapter covers language related to discussing health practices and making good choices in eating and behavior. Cultural themes in the chapter are tied to practices of various French speakers who try to maintain healthy lifestyles. Therefore, an overview for this IPA that expands on the idea of examining access to healthy food among underrepresented French speakers in the francophone world could be: "Students complete tasks that allow them to compare and contrast access to healthy foods and issues of food insecurity in four francophone countries and to offer possible solutions for addressing the issues."

3. Review your existing activities: Review your curriculum for interpretive (reading and listening), interpersonal (speaking and writing) and presentational (speaking and writing) activities related to the overview you have chosen for the IPA you already have students do. These activities can inspire the IPA tasks. For example, students might currently watch a series of short interviews in Spanish with bilingual Spanish-English speakers on a variety of topics and then answer comprehension questions (see http://www.coerll.utexas.edu/spintx for

Table 4.3. Modifications to Existing Assessments

Assessment	Type of Modification	Description
Reading comprehension assessment: Multiple choice comprehension questions based on a short poem in the target language	Alter	The original poem is changed to a poem written by an author from an underrepresented community. A mixture of multiple-choice and short answer ques-tions is used to assess students' comprehension.
Reading comprehension assessment: Draw a series of pictures from an adapted reader that demonstrate students' knowledge of the story	Alter	Draw a series of pictures from the point of view of a minor character or an animal in the story to demon-strate students' knowledge of the story and inspire conversation about the importance of perspectives.
Vocabulary assessment: Students match pictures and vocabulary terms from a word bank	Extend	After completing the first part of the quiz, students must use 10 vocabulary words and 6 verbs from the word bank in a paragraph describing their opinions on a topic related to social justice, to show their un-derstanding and application of vocabulary.
Verb conjugation assessment: Students must fill in the blank with the correct form or tense of a verb	Alter	Students must show that they can express meaning by using verbs in contextualized sentences about the work or mission of an advocacy organization.

examples). The new task can be watching videos more targeted to issues relating to social justice, such as iden-tity, education, and language. Students can then build on those interpretive activities to compare the themes with themes in poetry, essays, and other authentic texts.

Your Turn!

Use the table on the right to organize activities related to the theme of your IPA and begin to develop the tasks for various modes of communication depending on your instructional approach

Existing Activities Connected to Your IPA Theme/Overview
Example: Students read a cultural blurb about the different tracks of the education system and identify what kinds of careers they can obtain through each track.
Mode of Communication (Interpretive, Interpersonal or Presentational)
Example: Interpretive
Possible Task
Example: Students read an infographic that represents the number of native-born students in each track in comparison with the number of refugee and immigrant students in each track. Students compare and contrast these numbers and evaluate the extent to which the education system provides equitable access for students of all backgrounds.

Now that you have examined your curriculum for themes and activities that can be used to build your authentic summative assessments, you will be able to develop the tasks that fit with your current curriculum or an existing unit you teach. Below is an example of an *Integrated*

Performance Assessment that corresponds to the French lesson introduced in this chapter. (The IPA for the Spanish unit can be found in the full unit plan at the end of the chapter.)

Now it's your turn to create the tasks of IPA that correspond to your curriculum. You should use the ideas you created in the table in the previous activity as starting points for your work.

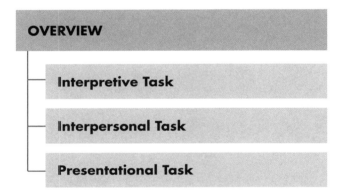

Steps 4 and 5: Create Key Formative Assessments and Learning Activities

When you work with an existing unit you teach, the process of developing formative assessment tasks and other learning activities will not be the same as the brainstorming process a teacher undergoes when writing an original unit. We recommend you begin your lesson planning by examining the areas of your existing unit or textbook chapter you are adapting. Then search for activities that will engage students in the topic and allow them to meet the unit goals you identified in Step 2 above. If you are using a textbook or other publisher-supplied materials, feel free to adapt some of your source's ideas and change them to make them your own. You need not use the activities and materials as written; again, you can alter, expand, or replace them, as you did with the summative assessments. You must, however, ensure that each activity you choose aligns with your goals and the standards.

Next, create original activities to use in this unit. In addition to existing activities you may have adapted, get creative and brainstorm learning and instructional activities that would engage your students in this unit's topic. Remember, you will align both the existing and the original activities to the social justice takeaway understandings and unit goals you identified in Step 2. Also, keep in mind that Steps 3 and 4 are recursive. You can go back-and-forth between them, making changes to the assessments based on the types of instructional activities you choose. Finally, in Step 5, you will write your daily lesson plans using your developed activities and assessments. Chapter 5 will include further detail on developing your key formative assessments and writing daily lesson plans.

Though you may still use your existing curriculum in its current form, you may find yourself examining your curriculum more often for social justice entry points. Adapting your existing curriculum to include topics of social justice has the potential to add depth, meaning and importance to what students are learning. We encourage you to seek out entry points in whichever kind of curriculum and instruction approach you use and to take advantage of them when you find them.

Conclusion

In this chapter, we propose that you do not necessarily need to start from scratch to create a communicative, contextualized unit that emphasizes social justice. Often your existing curriculum contains multiple entry points. As a teacher, you can use certain existing activities in the textbook or other curriculum materials that fit well with the unit, adapt existing activities to align them with the goals of your unit, or develop new, original activities for your unit. You may even find it easier to adapt an existing unit than to create your own from scratch, because of the ideas and inspiration your current curriculum can provide. At the end of the chapter, you can examine the entire unit frame for both the French adapted textbook chapter example and the Spanish content-based instruction example. Viewing these examples of unit frames may give you some ideas of what you can do with your own curriculum.

French (Novice-Mid to Novice-High) Integrated Performance Assessment

Healthy Lifestyles around the World

OVERVIEW: Students complete tasks that allow them to examine access to healthy foods and issues of food insecurity in four francophone countries and to offer possible solu-tions for addressing the issues.

Interpretive Tasks:

Students view short video clips about food desserts in the cities of Montréal and Paris and compare and contrast details about each using a Coggle mind map.

Students read a webpage about dependence on farming in Senegal and the risk of food insecurity during drought, summarizing the main issues.

Students watch a short video about food insecurity in Haiti and de-scribe the issues faced by Haitians and steps they take to access food.

Interpersonal Task: In small groups of four, students are tasked with comparing and con-trasting the needs of the four countries in order for the people in those countries to maintain their health. Students must also offer at least one solution. Together they fill in a graphic organizer; each group is digitally recorded.

Presentational Task: Students create their own infographic describing the healthy practices and needs of people in the four francophone countries, along with possi-ble solutions for addressing food insecurity and access to healthy foods.

Figure 4.2. An overview of an IPA in French related to health

Discussion Questions

1. What are some of the advantages of using publish-er-supplied materials as a foundation for your unit planning? What are some of the disadvantages of start-ing with existing materials? Name at least two of each.

2. If you use a textbook, answer this question: What are other social justice issues that would relate to common themes in textbooks? Would you classify them as pri-marily addressing products, practices, or perspectives? We have listed a few common themes at three different levels of traditional textbooks. Identify at least one social justice issue that you could explore at each level based on these provided themes.

   Level I Textbooks (Novice-Low to Novice-Mid rating on the *ACTFL Proficiency Guidelines*)

   a. School: Classes, supplies and materials, schedules

   b. House: Furniture, rooms, chores

   c. Clothing: Shopping, clothing items, colors, styles

   Level 2 Textbooks (Novice-Mid to Novice-High on the *ACTFL Proficiency Guidelines*)

   a. Health: Illnesses, going to the doctor

   b. Travel: Hotel, transportation

   c. City: Places found in a city, leisure-time activities

   Level 3 Textbooks (Novice-High to Intermediate-Low on *ACTFL Proficiency Guidelines*)

   a. Education and Work: Professions, education system

   b. Relationships: Family, friends, marriage, divorce

   c. Environment: Recycling, responsibilities, natural and manmade disasters

3. If you teach with a focus on comprehensible input, a content-driven approach, or in an immersion program, examine several of the readers you use or a few of your thematic units. Write down some of its content and features you believe particularly support social justice education. Write down content and features you think would be harder to adapt to support social justice education. How can you reconcile the two to integrate topics of social justice into one of your existing units?

4. Examine the two unit frames at the end of the chapter. What are some strengths of each of the units? Which aspects of them might you change if you were teaching the unit? Which features of these units give you some ideas for adaptations you could make to chapters or units you teach?

REFERENCES

Bex, M. (2015). What is a target structure? *The Comprehensible Classroom.* Retrieved from https://martinabex.com/2015/11/22/what-is-a-target-structure/

Chiariello, E. (May/June 2017). A classics debate. *Literacy Today,* 34(6), 26-29.

Doehla, D. (2011). *Using Project-Based Learning to Teach World Languages.* Retrieved from http://www.edutopia.org/blog/world-language-project-based-learning-education-curriculum-don-doehla

Einfeld, A., & Collins, D. (2010). The relationships between service-learning, social justice, multicultural competence, and civic engagement. *Journal of College Student Development,* 49(2), 95-109.

Fortune, T. W., Wieland, M., and MMIC Team. (2012). Adaptation of Engineering is Elementary® "Model Membrane" Unit. Retrieved from: http://carla.umn.edu/immersion/MMIC/unit_membranes.html

Fortune, T. W., & Tedick, D. J. (2008). One-way, two-way and indigenous immersion: A call for cross-fertilization. In T. W. Fortune & D. J. Tedick (Eds.), *Pathways to multilingualism: Evolving perspectives on immersion education* (pp. 3–21). Clevedon: Multilingual Matters.

Hastings, A. (2012). *MovieTalk: Preview.* Retrieved from http://glesismore.com/movietalk/preview.html

High Quality Project-Based Learning (2018). Retrieved from https://hqpbl.org/wp-content/uploads/2018/03/FrameworkforHQPBL.pdf

Kaye, C. B. (2010). The complete guide to service learning: Proven, practical ways to engage students in civic responsibility, academic curriculum, and social action. Minneapolis, MN: Free Spirit Publishing.

Met. M. (1999, January). *Content-based instruction: Defining terms, making decisions.* NFLC Reports. Washington, DC: The National Foreign Language Center.

Met, M. (1999). "Making Connections." In: June B. Phillips (ed.) *Foreign Language Standards: Linking Research, Theories, and Practices.* Lincolnwood, IL: National Textbook Co.

The National Standards Collaborative Board. (2015). *World-Readiness Standards for Learning Languages.* 4th ed. Alexandria, VA: Author.

Schmitt, C. J., & Brillié Lutz, K. (2007). *Glencoe French 2: Bon Voyage!* New York: Glencoe/McGraw Hill.

Shrum, J., & Glisan, E. W. (2010) *Teacher's handbook: Contextualized language instruction* (4th Ed.) Boston, MA: Heinle.

Tedick, D. J., & Wesely, P. M. (2015). A review of research on content-based foreign/second language education in US K-12 contexts. *Language, Culture and Curriculum,* 28(1), 25-40.

Wiggins, G. & McTighe, J. (2005). *Understanding by design* (2nd ed.). Alexandria, VA: Assn. for Supervision & Curriculum Development.

Introductory Materials for Comprehensible Input

Bex, M. (2015). *The comprehensible classroom.* Retrieved from https://martinabex.com/

Ray, B., & Seely, C. (1997). *Fluency through TPR storytelling: Achieving real language acquisition in school* (5th Ed.). Berkeley, CA: Command Performance Language Institute.

Slavic, B. & Hargarden, T. (2017). *A natural approach to stories: A happier way to teach languages.* Auburn Hills, MI: Teacher's Discovery.

Suggested Spanish-Language Leveled Readers with Social Justice Themes

Canion, Mira – *Fiesta Fatal*

Degenhart, Jennifer – *Los tres amigos*

Degenhart, Jennifer – *La niñera*

Degenhart, Jennifer – *La chica nueva*

Gaab, Carol – *Felipe Alou* (also available in French)

Gaab, Carol – *Esperanza*

Hildebrandt, Virginia – *Soy Lorenzo*

Placido, Kristy – *Vidas impactantes*

See also work by Rachelle Adams and Anna Gilcher

Novice High Level French Unit Frame Adapted from the Level 2 Textbook *Bon Voyage!* (Schmitt & Brillié Lutz, 2007)

Theme and Essential Question(s)

Healthy Lifestyles around the World – *How can culture and access impact one's health both positively and negatively? How I can support myself and others in maintaining a healthy lifestyle?*

Social Justice Takeaway Understanding(s)

- There are numerous views of a healthy lifestyle in the francophone world.
- The ability to maintain a healthy lifestyle depends on access (to healthcare, clean water, fresh food, etc.) and socioeco-nomic status.
- Empowerment of individuals in their own communities can lead to sustainable sources of fresh foods and income.

Goals

- Students will be able to describe their own efforts and others' efforts to maintain a healthy lifestyle in four franco-phone countries (France, Canada, Senegal, Haiti) using vocabulary and reflexive verbs.
- Students will be able to explain how access to resources and socioeconomic status affect the health and lifestyles of people in the four francophone countries.
- Students will be able to compare and contrast access to resources in these four countries to their own communities and cultures.
- Students will be able to identify the way in which Heifer International and other organizations support communities in need with sustainable practices that lead to agency among the members of the community.
- Students will be able to create a Heifer International campaign (in the target language) for their school to buy re-sources for a francophone community in need.

World-Readiness Standards

Communication:
- Interpersonal, Interpretive, Presentational

Cultures:
- Practices to Perspectives: Understanding the ways in which different people in different cultures participate in trying to maintain their health
- Products to Perspectives: Examination of resources available in students' own culture and target cultures

Connections:
- Making Connections: Link to what students have learned previously in Health classes
- Acquiring Information and Diverse Perspectives: Authentic videos that show how people live in the four francophone countries being explored

Comparisons:
- Language Comparisons: Reflexive verbs in French and English
- Cultural Comparisons: Comparisons of health practices and daily lives of people in the U.S. and in fran-cophone countries

Communities:
- School and Global Communities: Schoolwide Heifer International campaign
- Lifelong Learning: Understanding the difference be-tween donation and empowering others in communities in need.

Teaching Tolerance Social Justice Standards

Diversity:
- Students will develop language and knowledge to accurately and respectfully describe how people (including themselves) are both similar to and different from each other and others in their identity groups.

Justice:
- Students will recognize that power and privilege influence relationships on interpersonal, intergroup and institutional levels and consider how they themselves have been affected by those dynamics.

Summative Assessments

Interpretive Communication
- Students view short video clips about food deserts in the cities of Montréal and Paris and compare and contrast de-tails about each using a Coggle mind map.
- Students read a webpage about dependence on farming in Senegal and the risk of food insecurity during drought, summarizing the main issues.
- Students watch a short video about food insecurity in Haiti and describe the issues faced by Haitians and the steps they take to access food.

Interpersonal Communication
- In small groups of 4, students are tasked with comparing and contrasting the needs of the four countries in order for the people in those coun-tries to maintain their health. Together they fill in a graphic organizer; each group is digitally recorded.

Presentational Communication
- Students create their own infographic that describes the healthy practices and needs of people in the four francophone countries.

Intermediate-Low Level Spanish Content-Based Instruction Unit Frame (Written by Talía González)

Theme and Essential Question(s)

Latino Civil Rights — *What are civil rights? Who were important Latino civil rights leaders and what kind of impact did they have? What are some modern civil rights issues that are important to Latinos? How have Latinos in the U.S. contributed to the fight for civil rights?*

Social Justice Takeaway Understanding(s)

- The challenges faced by oppressed groups are structural in nature.
- Both the oppressed and privileged have the ability to effect change for oppressed groups and individuals.

Goals

- Students will be able to discuss what it means to be bicultural and/or bilingual, along with its benefits and challenges.
- Students will be able to present information on important Latino leaders and what they did to effect change.
- Students will be able to analyze the challenges Latinos face and discuss the need for powerful leaders to face these challenges.
- Students will be able to comprehend how the Latino experience has changed over time.
- Students will be able to describe important events that affect Latinos today.
- Students will be able to analyze literature born out of the U.S. Latino experience.

World-Readiness Standards

Communication:
- Interpersonal, Interpretive, Presentational

Cultures:
- Practices to Perspectives: Latinos' acts to affect change and their beliefs
- Products to Perspectives: Literature and other artifacts that represent Latinos' experiences in the U.S.

Connections:
- Making Connections: Social Studies—Draw on what students are learning about civil rights in the U.S.; English Language Arts—Analysis of literature and formal letter writing
- Acquiring Information and Diverse Perspectives: Literature and other text written by Latinos in and outside of the U.S.

Comparisons:
- Language Comparisons: Grammatical concepts like comparatives and direct and indirect object pronouns; vocabulary related to professions
- Cultural Comparisons: Comparing and contrasting their own childhood and education experiences with those of immigrant Latinos.

Communities:
- School and Global Communities: Invite guest speakers who are dreamers to form a panel
- Lifelong Learning: Development of empathy and understanding of Latinos' experiences

Teaching Tolerance Social Justice Standards

Identity:
- Students will develop language and historical and cultural knowledge that affirm and accurately describe their membership in multiple identity groups.
- Students will recognize that people's multiple identities interact and create unique and complex individuals.

Diversity:
- Students will develop language and knowledge to accurately and respectfully describe how people (including themselves) are both similar to and different from each other and others in their identity groups.

Justice:
- Students will recognize that power and privilege influence relationships on interpersonal, intergroup and institutional levels and consider how they have been affected by those dynamics.
- Students will identify figures, groups, events and a variety of strategies and philosophies relevant to the history of social justice around the world

Action:
- Students will speak up with courage and respect when they or someone else has been hurt or wronged by bias.

Summative Assessments

Interpretive Communication
- Students listen to several clips of Latinos who describe in Spanish their experiences as immigrant children in the U.S. Students create a word cloud to represent the experiences shared in the clips.
- Students read bios about important Latinos who fought for justice and effected change in the U.S. in the face of tremendous structural challenges. Some examples include Sylvia Méndez, César Chávez, and Dolores Huerta. Students compare and contrast details about each individual, looking for commonalities in their bios, but also unique traits and actions.

Interpersonal Communication
- Students interview each other about their own childhood and experiences, asking each other to compare their childhood to those of the Latinos they learned about in the interpretive task.

Presentational Communication
- Students pretend that they are teaching a third-grade unit about civil rights in a Spanish immersion school and need to help the third graders understand important cases like Méndez vs. Westminster that have taken place. They choose one case and have to include important details that took place and explain why the case was significant. They can use any tools to make it engaging and interesting for third graders.
- Students choose an issue significant to the Latino community in the U.S. and write a formal letter in Spanish to a politician to share their opinion on the topic.

CHAPTER 5
Planning Daily Lessons

This chapter will guide you in creating effective lessons to be used within your social justice unit. If you are a pre-service teacher, this will enable you to think about the specifics of what will occur in your classroom, including what you will do, what the students will do, and the resources and materials you will need to engage your learners in a robust learning experience. If you are an in-service teacher, this section will enable you to think deeply about aligning your lesson objectives, planned activities and assessments while incorporating social justice themes and understandings.

A Glimpse into the Classroom

It is the last day of back-to-school preplanning for Li, Elena, and their departmental colleagues at Franklin High. Now that they have created the framework for an identity-themed unit, they have decided to move to lesson planning. After an intense brainstorming session, they reached consensus on a few key instructional activities that will support their students in reaching the social justice and language objectives they planned. Regardless of the target language, each teacher plans to engage her or his students in a similar problem-posting activity.

Students will analyze stereotypical images depicting an individual from the target culture. All images will be authentic and found in US popular culture texts. For instance, Li uses the images and video clips of two Siamese cat characters from the *Rescue Rangers* cartoon series. The cats are depicted as Asian characters who own a Laundromat and have an illegal gambling operation in a basement. Elena begins with an illustration of Speedy González, a mouse depicted in a Mexican sombrero. Samira chooses a video clip from the 1992 movie *Aladdin,* which includes an Arab merchant character depicted as greedy, menacing, and violent. The other teachers work together to find images on the Internet representing individuals from their target cultures.

The teachers plan to then guide students in unpacking the stereotypes and assumptions in the racist depictions. To scaffold this, the teachers create a list of carefully planned questions and tasks (e.g., *Describe the features of this image that you believe to be stereotypical*) and a graphic organizer that will help the students organize their thoughts. They also brainstorm anticipated student responses to the questions.

Finally, the students will analyze the cases of actual adolescents living in their target cultures of instruction, based on YouTube videos, Instagram or Twitter profiles, Facebook pages, or other authentic, media-based texts the teachers find. The purpose of this final part of the activity is to reframe students' thinking about the connections among nationality, culture and the intersectional nature of identity. They will then contrast characteristics of their "new friends" from the target culture with the pop-culture-based depictions in the target language.

Now that you have read the vignette, answer these questions:

1. What will the teachers need to think about in preparation for the problem-posing activity? What elements should they include in their plans?

2. What additional materials will the teachers need for the activity to be successful?

3. The vignette notes, "Students will analyze stereotypical images depicting an individual from a selected target culture." What specific questions could the teachers ask their students during the lesson to engage them in this type of analysis?

4. What type of extension activity could the teachers create that would engage students in action related to the social justice issues they have investigated?

The Relationship between Unit and Lesson Planning

In Chapters 3 and 4, we discussed big-picture planning, which you do when you write curriculum maps, create plan units, or change unit themes during the school year. Remember, we conceptualized a unit plan as a long-range plan that typically incorporates several weeks of lessons around a specific theme and a takeaway understanding related to social justice. Figure 5.1 illustrates the way your planning should flow, from the big picture to your more focused daily lesson plans.

Lesson plans enable teachers to think through their decision-making about "where they will go" with their students before they step into the classroom. Ultimately, lesson planning should stimulate you to think about your intended outcomes, plan a structure and roadmap for the lesson, foresee problems that might occur, and keep a record of what was taught (Richards, 1998).

Although some researchers and authors conceptualize a lesson as spanning up to a few days, in this chapter we define **a lesson** as a daily plan spanning one instructional period. At this point, particularly if you are a novice or pre-service teacher, you may want to use a lesson-planning template, which will help you stay organized as you plan. A variety of lesson planning formats ranging in structure, emphasis, and level of detail are available. For a more detailed template geared specifically to planning for world languages, see Appendix K of Clementi & Terrill's (2017) *The Keys to Planning for Learning: Effective Curriculum, Unit, and Lesson Design.*

Some teachers write very detailed plans; others have the more specific parts of their plans in their heads. Regardless of whether you are a novice or veteran teacher, you must think in advance about what you will do and what you want your students to do, particularly when you add a social justice layer to your language lessons. In this chapter we describe a process for writing **long-form lesson plans,** which are highly detailed and are typically used in teacher education programs. Most of all, they encourage teachers to think carefully about all aspects of the lesson. However, we recognize that in-service teachers will not necessarily write everything out in such detail. Nevertheless, even

Figure 5.1. A flowchart for planning

in-service teachers will want to note some of the new elements we recommend for inclusion in a lesson that incorporates social justice understandings.

Steps to an Effective, Useful Lesson Plan
Step 1: Select the Standards to Be Prioritized in the Lesson

Your first step will be to identify the standard or standards that will provide your lesson's starting point and framework. At this point you will have identified the standards that will shape your unit. Now you must choose the specific standard or standards that will drive your lesson for that particular day. You *do not* have to meet all of the unit standards in each and every lesson. Use the *World-Readiness Standards* (The National Standards Collaborative Board, 2015) and the *Social Justice Standards* (Teaching Tolerance, 2016) as a starting point for your work. Beginning with the World-Readiness Standards (WRS), you might envision a lesson that focuses most heavily on interpretive communication and the comparisons standard related to comparing cultures. You could also review the standards related to "identity" in the Social Justice Standards (SJS) framework as inspiration.

Step 2: Select the Objectives to Be Prioritized in the Lesson

It is now time to decide what you want your students to be able to do by the end of the instructional period. These objectives should connect with the standards you intend to emphasize during the lesson. For world languages teachers who see their students for a short period each day, such as a 30-minute or 45-minute period, one or two objectives will suffice for the lesson plan, and even be ambitious! Teachers with a longer amount of instructional time may be able to plan for more than one or two objectives. However, we caution you to be conservative in the number of objectives; focus instead on students' ability to successfully meet the objective by the end of the instructional period. We have seen many examples of lesson plans that included four or five objectives and focused on breadth rather than depth. Conversely, we have seen examples of other plans with one strong objective students were able to accomplish with independence by the end of the period. You may focus on the same objective for several days to ensure students reach such independence. Ultimately, we want all of our students to gain such independence as a result of our instruction.

Your learning objectives should be **functional** in nature, describing what learners will be able to do in the target language and culture (Shrum & Glisan, 2016). Objectives should be meaningful and connected to the ways we use language authentically in real life, hence not focused on specific grammar points. Rather than stating, "Students will be able to conjugate regular -ar, -er, and -ir verbs in the future tense," focus on what students would be able to *do* with such verbs. This objective could be changed to "Students will be able to describe five things they will do to raise awareness of environmental justice." This marks a shift in the fundamental purpose for teaching grammar. It is not "grammar for grammar's sake," but grammar instruction that becomes a means for authentic, meaningful communication. Supporting students to notice meaning and structure is part of input. It also enables you to create a social justice context for student learning.

Objectives should include clear action verbs—describe, identify, compare, list, circle, write, label, etc.—and should articulate the result. In addition, objectives should be mea-surable; you should be able to assess or evaluate the extent to which individual students accomplished them. Finally, your objectives should not include language related to a specific activity. For instance, rather than stating, "Students will be able to describe their identities in a simulation activity," a stronger objective would be, "Students will be able to describe their identities." The information detailing the activities you will use to reach your destination (the objective) will be evident in your lesson plans, where you will list your teaching and learning activities.

Now it's your turn to choose at least *one lesson objective* related to a social justice outcome for an original lesson plan that would fit within a unit you began in Chapter 3 or Chapter 4. If you are struggling with this, revisit the Social Justice Standards, listed in Chapter 1. As an alternative, you can write an objective for the lesson Li and his colleagues began planning in the vignette at the beginning of the chapter. Make sure your objective is aligned with the social justice and language objectives you indicated in your unit plan outline.

WRS & SJS Standard(s) Addressed in Lesson	Social Justice Objective Addressed in Lesson

Now, use the questions below to perform a self-check of your work so far:

- Is the objective aligned with your standards and your planned unit social justice and/or language objectives?

- Does it use strong, observable action verbs, not vague verbs like "learn" and "understand"?

- Does it avoid naming specific grammar points (e.g., the past tense of the verb "to be")?

- Is it meaningful for students?

Table 5.1. Novice Mid-Novice High Unit Frame

Theme and Essential Question(s)

Identity – *What makes up one's identity?*

Social Justice Takeaway Understanding(s)

Our identities are multifaceted, intersectional, and connected to experiences and membership in different social groups.

Goals

- Students will be able to describe elements of their identity, including physical characteristics, membership in different social groups, and personal qualities.
- Students will be able to compare and contrast personal characteristics and qualities with their others.
- Students will be able to ask and tell about origin and nationality.
- Students will be able to explain why images from the target culture are stereotypical and do not appropriately describe an individual's identity.
- Students will be able to define the concept of microaggressions and provide two examples in the target language.

World-Readiness Standards	Teaching Tolerance Social Justice Standards
Communication: - Interpersonal, Interpretive, Presentational **Cultures:** - Practices to Perspectives: Cultural practices that are central and important to identity - Products to Perspectives: Characteristics that are central and important to identity **Connections:** - Making Connections: Geography—locations and ethnic backgrounds of speakers of the TL - Acquiring Information and Diverse Perspectives: Reading short bios and watching short videos about people from the target culture in different roles in their communities **Comparisons:** - Language Comparisons: Adjectives, geographical locations, ethnicities - Cultural Comparisons: Comparing and contrasting students' own identities to bios of people in the target culture they learn about **Communities:** - School and Global Communities: Students learn about each others' identities, sharing and building community with each other in their classroom. - Lifelong Learning: Students will recognize stereotypes for what they are and see beyond them.	**Identity:** - Students will develop positive social identities based on their membership in multiple groups in society. - Students will develop language and historical and cultural knowledge that affirm and accurately describe their membership in multiple identity groups. **Justice:** - Students will recognize stereotypes and relate to people as individuals rather than representatives of groups.

- Is it assessable?

- Does it avoid naming specific activities?

You should be able to answer "yes" to each of these questions. Revisit any questions for which your answer was "no" for further reflection. For instance, for Li and his colleagues' "All About Me" unit, the department first returned to their unit frame, including the unit standards and unit objectives (Table 5.1).

The team had planned four communicative, language-based goals and two social justice goals that were clearly related to the language objectives and grounded in their context and their students' specific needs. Because their unit would be taught in a Novice-Mid classroom in

the first quarter of the school year, they did not expect students to meet all goals in the target language. Yet they knew the students would be able to use the target language during some social justice learning activities.

To plan the lessons for the unit, the team chose the objectives they hoped students would meet each day, paying attention to both language and social justice objectives. The teachers began to sketch out the specific lesson objectives for each day and came up with the list in Table 5.2. Note that each objective mirrors one of their unit objectives, and that some objectives span more than one day. (The All About Me unit plan in its entirety, including formative assessments and daily lesson plan objectives, can be found in Appendix C.)

Table 5.2. The Department's List of Daily Objectives

Day #	Objective
Day 1	Students will be able to describe their physical characteristics and personal qualities.
Day 2	Students will be able to describe their physical characteristics and personal qualities as well as those that others assume about them.
Day 3	Students will be able to describe their physical characteristics and personal qualities, noting the areas where there are intersections.
Day 4	Students will be able to tell their age and ask a friend her or his age.
Day 5	Students will be able to compare and contrast their ages and physical characteristics with others. Students define microaggressions and provide examples in the target language.
Day 6	Students will be able to tell someone where they are from.
Day 7	Students will be able to tell someone their age and where they are from.
Day 8	Students will be able to compare their geographical origins with the geographical origins of others.
Day 9	Students will be able to compare where they are from with the geographical origins of others.
Day 10	Students will be able to analyze the stereotypes inherent in images of people from the target culture.
Day 11	Students will be able to explain why images from the target culture do not appropriately describe an individual's identity.
Days 12–15	Integrated Performance Assessment

Now it's your turn to think through how each lesson in your unit will address at least one objective you outlined. Copy the simple chart below onto a piece of paper with the objective for every day. Add days for each day of your unit.

Day #	Objective
Day 1	
Day 2	
Day 3	

Step 3: Create or Identify Formative Assessments

In Chapter 3, we distinguished between summative and formative assessments. Formative assessments, designed to evaluate students' knowledge and skills as the unit progresses, enable teachers to reflect on their students' progress and make adjustments as necessary to clarify points or hone their students' skills further (Shrum & Glisan, 2016). Formative assessments may be **informal** (a task that is non-graded, like oral questioning, an interpersonal activity you observe to determine how students are progressing, or an exit card) or **formal** (something handed in by students or graded) to allow the teacher and students to gauge students' comprehension. When formative assessments are authentic, such as responding to websites from the target culture or writing a short email, they can both connect with social justice issues and expose students to authentic language.

Many teachers wait to consider what they will use to formatively assess students until *after* they have planned a lesson's activities. However, when you determine an effective, informative assessment for a lesson at the beginning of your planning, be sure to build it into the activities at an appropriate point in the lesson. Remember that any assessment used should be **valid**—it should accurately measure your objective for the lesson—and viewed as a **tool** that enables you to collect valuable **evidence,** or **data,** about student learning in light of your planned objective(s). This tool should be the product of the assessment and should be useful data to you as a teacher.

Important questions to consider here include:

- To what extent can I make my formative assessments authentic?

- How do the formative assessments gauge students' ability to meet the language and social justice objectives of the lesson?

- What formative assessments can I use to prepare students for the summative assessment?

For instance, Li and his colleagues brainstormed at least one formative assessment for each day of instruction, listed below. They made sure that the assessments were valid and aligned with each lesson objective. They also made sure each assessment included a tool for analyzing the extent to which each student in the class met the lesson objective for that day. In other words, they had a way of gauging the learning of the individual students in their class each day. They could then use this information to go back and re-teach material to specific groups of students who needed additional support. They were also careful to consider how each formative assessment would build toward the summative assessment at the end of the unit.

Notice that the formative assessments listed double as teaching and learning activities. This represents an integrated approach to teaching and assessment, rather than assessment as an add-on that neglects to expand student learning. The examples in the next table provide some additional ideas for formative assessments that could be used in each unit. Although they are targeted toward Spanish, French, and German classrooms, think of how you could adapt them for your target language.

Table 5.3. The Department's List of Objectives and Formative Assessments

Mode of Communication and Objective	Formative Assessments
Students will be able to describe their physical characteristics and personal qualities. *Presentational Communication*	**Teacher Checklist:** Observation of Total Physical Response (TPR) performance for eight (8) adjectives related to identity markers. **Student Self-Evaluation Checklist Exit Ticket:** How many new words can I identify? How many can I use?
Students will be able to describe their physical characteristics and personal qualities as well as those that others assume about them. *Presentational Communication* *Interpersonal Communication*	**Adapted Circles of My Multicultural Self:** Students complete two versions of the Circles Activity (see Chapter 2): one based on what others assume about them, and one based on their actual identity elements. **Assumptions or truths:** Students use the circles activity to ask each other about elements of their identities, providing yes/no answers about the assumptions and truths.
Students will be able to describe their physical characteristics and personal qualities, noting the areas where there are intersections. *Presentational Communication* *Interpersonal Communication*	**Peer Characteristics Scavenger Hunt:** Students walk around and write names of classmates on a worksheet who fit the identity markers on the worksheet. **"I am . . ." Presentational Writing:** Students write short statements and include a collage/visual representation, emphasizing areas of intersection.
Students will be able to tell their age and ask a friend his/her age. *Interpersonal Communication*	**Teacher Checklist:** Could they do it? 30-second partner performance-based assessment.
Students will be able to compare and contrast their ages and physical characteristics with others. Students define microaggressions and provide an example in the target language. *Interpretive Communication* *Presentational Communication*	**Characteristics Venn Diagram:** Students read one of their classmates' "I am" from projects from Day 2 and compare their characteristics with those of two of their classmates. **Microaggression Examples Poster:** After watching a short video about microaggressions, students brainstorm some microaggressions in the target language. In their L1, they explain why they are hurtful, insensitive, or stereotypical. The poster becomes the basis for a hallway display to teach other students about microaggressions.
Students will be able to tell someone where they are from. *Interpretive Communication* *Presentational Communication*	**Social Justice (SJ) Heroes:** Posters depicting the name, country of origin and characteristics of various social justice leaders will be hung around the room. Students walk around and write a statement about where they are from. **Tech-Oral Exit Ticket:** Students tweet or Instagram a picture and statement about where they are from and then say the statement on the way out.
Students will be able to tell someone their age and where they are from. *Interpersonal Communication*	**Teacher Checklist:** Could they do it? 15-second individual performance assessment.
Students will be able to compare their geographical origins with those of others. *Interpretive Communication* *Presentational Communication*	**Homework Comparison Table:** Create a comparison chart of origins based on the results of the in-class interpersonal communicative activity and social justice poster activity from earlier in the unit. They calculate class-wide percentages of individuals representing different ethnicities, ages, and some additional identity markers.
Students will be able to compare where they are from with the geographical origins of others. *Presentational Communication*	**All About Me Technology-Based Project:** Students use various forms of technology (differentiated as appropriate) to create an "all about me" illustration. This is assessed with a mini-project rubric.
Students will be able to analyze the stereotypes inherent in images of people from the target culture. *Interpretive Communication*	**Before-and-After Survey and Reflection:** Students complete a Perceptions and Stereotypes survey (in their L1) prior to the lesson and after the lesson. They then analyze their own growth.
Students will be able to explain why images from the target culture do not appropriately describe an individual's identity. *Presentational Communication*	**Image Description:** In groups, students write and then present 3–4 statements describing the individual's or image's characteristics (in TL). **Problem-Posing Analysis and Reflection:** Students analyze the possible stereotypes in their image. They present this in their L1 on a poster. With a poster carousel, groups add to posters with additional thoughts.

Your Turn!

Now it's your turn to develop a list of potential formative assessments for your lessons. Copy the chart below with the objective for every day and the formative assessments you think will work best. Add as many days as you have planned for the unit.

Day #	Formative Assessments
Day 1	
Day 2	
Day 3	

Step 4: Brainstorm Lesson Activities

Now is the time for you to harness your creativity and plan the route that will transport students to their destination. The first step will be to think through a variety of appropriate activities that might work. If you don't use them in this lesson, you might use them in another. To brainstorm, we suggest you gather a few materials and resources:

- A blank piece of paper or computer screen;

- A list of the key language (vocabulary and functions) students will need to succeed in your unit;

- The work you did in Steps 2 (Objectives) and 3 (Formative Assessments) in plotting out each day of your unit; and

Table 5.4. Additional Formative Assessment Examples for Spanish, French, Chinese, and German

---

Spanish I (Novice-Mid) Formative Assessment Examples

Example 1: Latinos/as in Our School Interviews. Half of the students will be assigned the role of the reporter who is doing a story on *Latinos en nuestro colegio* (Latinos in our school) and the way that they choose to identify in terms of their race, ethnicity, or country of origin. The other half of students will be given a card with a map of all Spanish-speaking countries with one highlighted. After exchanging greetings, reporters will ask students if they are Latino/a; partners will answer either "yes" or "no," indicate their country of origin, and preferred identity label. Re-porters will write down their partners' names and ethnicity labels on a worksheet.

Example 2: Video Interpretation. Students will watch a short teacher-created video that features three adoles-cent immigrants from the community from different Spanish-speaking countries. As they watch, they will use a graphic organizer to jot down their names, ages, other personal descriptors, such as sex or gender, ethnicities, and countries of origin.

Example 3: Census Data Analysis and Interpretation Worksheet. Students will preview Census data charts similar to those they will see on the IPA, which include data related to the demographics of Spanish-speaking groups in the US. They will answer comprehension questions based on their analyses of the data on the charts and graphs.

French II (Novice-Mid to Novice-High) Formative Assessment Examples

Example 1: Profiles of Habits of French Speakers. Students receive profiles of French speakers from France, Senegal, and Hai-ti and must adopt this profile as their own. They engage in conversations with students from the other two countries to ask and answer questions about their eating habits. For example, what does someone in Senegal typically eat? What kinds of foods are easily found? Which foods are they unable to eat because they are unavail-able (due to issues of access)? What kinds of foods can they afford to buy?

Example 2: Preparation for The Heifer Project in Senegal and Haiti. Students examine the animals and resources on the *Heifer Project* website, identifying them in French. They choose the animals and resources most appropriate for Senegal and Haiti. Then, they describe the usefulness of the animal or the resource by creating a list of ways it could provide additional resources and sustain-ability for communities.

Example 3: Comprehending the Story of *Felipe Alou*. Students read the novel *Felipe Alou* (Gaab, 2014), about a non-English speaking black athlete from the Dominican Republic in the United States in the 1950s. They select from a set of activities designed to have them report on how they understand the chapter they have just read. They select from writing and answering their own compre-hension questions about the topic in French, summarizing the story with illustrations, or writing incorrect or false sentences in French and their corrected versions.

- The list of the categories of social justice activities we provided in Chapter One and Appendix A, which includes a table of potential social justice understandings, activities, and materials that can be adapted to a variety of languages and levels.

Using this information, list the possible learning activities that would be appropriate for your lesson. We recommend you use your own experiences as students, observers, and teachers to think through different activities that might work for your classroom context. To guide you in this process, ask yourself as you work:

- Which *modes of communication* (interpretive, interpersonal, presentational) are students using in these activities? Is there a good variety?

- What kinds of *authentic materials* can I access that might support the activity? How can students learn from those materials?

- Which *components of culture* (products, practices, perspectives) are students examining in these activities? Is there a good variety?

- Which *models of classroom organization* (whole-class, individual, groups, pairs) are used in these activities? Is there a good variety?

As you create your lesson activities, we encourage you to create a concept map, a table, or another type of graphic organizer that works best with your approach to instructional planning. We also encourage you to examine Appendix A, which includes examples of activities organized

Table 5.4. Additional Formative Assessment Examples for Spanish, French, Chinese, and German (continued)

Chinese 1 (Novice High) CI/TPRS Formative Assessment Examples (Original Ideas from Reed Riggs)

Example 1: PictureTalk. The teacher shows students pictures of people doing work for NGOs in China and graphs and charts showing statistics related to people in need. The teacher asks students a variety of questions to help them describe what they see in the pictures; new or unfamiliar vocabulary is posted with the translations. By the end of this activity, students will be able to state three things about a group that helps people (one in China and one in the U.S.). The teacher and students may choose to co-create a graphic organizer to house the students' ideas.

Example 2: Personalized Questions and Answers (PQA) or CardTalk. To examine the concept of "wants" versus "needs," students are asked to draw a few small pictures illustrating something they need to survive, something they would want in a hotel, and something they would want in a restaurant. The students can provide details about what is in the pictures, but mainly the teacher will ask yes/no or either/or questions about the students' pic-tures to help them determine differences between what they need and what they want.

Example 3: Story-Asking. The teacher provides a story in which the target structures are bolded while the variable details are underlined, allowing the students and teacher to co-create a new story about a marginalized group in need of access to resources. The main goal is to find an actionable, sustainable, real-world solution. Students follow the story-asking activity by creating a storyboard to represent the story and their solutions, which may vary from student to student, depending on individual ideas.

German III (Novice-High to Intermediate-Low) Formative Assessment Examples

Example 1: Gentrification of Berlin. Students watch a clip from YouTube about the way gentrification in Berlin is threatening historical landmarks, such as the East Side Gallery, a preserved section of the Berlin Wall. They follow this with a Webquest to compare and contrast gentrification in various areas of Berlin with gentrification in their own capital of Washington D.C.

Example 2: Voicethread Tour of Berlin. In pairs, students record their voices on voicethread.com to create their own tours of Berlin in which they focus on one particular area of the city and the people who live there. They should highlight gentrification that may have taken place and its influence on the people who live in that area of Berlin.

Example 3: Berliner Role Play. Students will be given an identity with information pertaining to their ethnicity, SES, religion, housing, community, etc. Students will partner and interview each other. A list of questions will be provided for them to ask. They will switch partners and complete the interview again. After the activity is complet-ed, the true identities will be revealed, allowing students to find out how their partners' backgrounds varied. Stu-dents will write a short synopsis of their partners' identities, noting the ways products, practices and perspectives intersect.

by theme. You are welcome to use the ideas in Appendix A, but we would also like to empower you to be creative and adapt them as necessary to design activities that will help your students meet the social justice and language objectives you plan.

Your Turn!

Now it's your turn to create a list of teaching and learning activities that will meet your objectives and lead to the formative assessments you have already developed. You can present your activities in any format, but try to stay focused on feasible, diverse activities.

Step 5: Sequence Your Lesson Activities

After identifying appropriate activities for your social justice lesson, you will need to verify that you are sequencing activities appropriately, to ensure that the learning activities in a given lesson are progressive and cohesive. For instance, just as you might introduce new language structures and vocabulary by emphasizing the receptive modalities (listening and reading) first, a social justice lesson should begin with exploration and investigation. That is, in most cases we would advise you to wait before you ask students to express opinions or analyze information about the social justice issues at hand. Luckily, this idea of exploration and investigation works well with receptive language activities, thus functions well in a world language classroom. Then, after the receptive activities, while continuing to address the same objectives, you can shift your students to a more productive aspect of the lesson, where they must process the material actively. At this point, they will also be better equipped to analyze information and express their opinions.

There are a few different ways you can structure your lesson to maximize student learning and use instructional time effectively and efficiently. We recommend the sequencing in the template plan in Appendix K of Clementi & Terrill's (2017) *The Keys to Planning for Learning: Effective Curriculum, Unit, and Lesson Design.* As this template illustrates, an appropriate sequence might be:

For my eighth graders, we learn about poverty, particularly in the Guatemalan town of Peña Blanca. Students gain awareness of the issue of poverty by watching a documentary, *Living on One* (2013), which features American college students who attempt to live in Peña Blanca with only $1 a day. The documentary usually takes about two 57-minute class periods. My students' eyes are opened to a different picture of poverty, one to which they have not been exposed."

— Carmel deGuzman, Spanish Teacher, Medford, New Jersey

1. Gain attention/activate prior knowledge

2. Provide input

3. Elicit performance/provide feedback

4. Provide input

5. Elicit performance/provide feedback

6. Closure

7. Enhance retention and transfer

Other structures for sequencing lessons are common in our field. One such classic structure is the **preview-view-review structure,** wherein the teacher "previews" an objective with the students through an inductive activity. Students get a hint of the class topic and are provided with some tools to process it. Then, in the "view" stage, the students are given direct instruction on the topic, with all components made explicit through direct instruction. Finally, the "review" portion of the lesson asks students to put their new knowledge to the test. In a social justice lesson, you might start by having students do a quick reading that features key vocabulary and concepts. Then you will present on the topic, asking them to take notes or complete a worksheet as you present. Finally, you will ask them to review what they have learned through a guided class discussion or performance task.

Regardless of your chosen structure, as you plan what you will do at each step of your lesson plan, you will undoubtedly go back and forth between Steps 3 (Formative Assessment) and 4 (Activities) in your lesson planning. You may need to adjust your assessments based on how you develop your learning activities, and vice-versa. Finally, you may not follow the lesson plan verbatim while enacting it, but thinking through each detail in advance will help you feel more organized and foresee any issues that could arise, particularly when trying out a social justice activity for the first time.

Now it's your turn to plan learning activities for your lesson plan. Using the template provided in Appendix D, or another preferred template or lesson structure, plan one lesson in detail, using some of the formative assessments and activities you developed in Steps 3 and 4.

Using Authentic Resources in Social Justice Themed Lessons

Sometimes we discover a great authentic image or another resource we want to use with students that is more relevant when used immediately rather than waiting to fit it into a unit. This becomes a stand-alone lesson. Other times this resource fits nicely into a lesson for a current unit or can inspire a theme of a new unit you want to create. The Internet and social media offer a wide variety of images, media-based photos, videos, audio, and other resources with rich social justice themes. One example is the array of signs that appeared worldwide in Women's Marches in January 2017. The messages in the signs revealed a multitude of cultural practices and perspectives on human rights, social justice, peace, democracy, equity, and other civic engagement-related issues. These signs also held clear connections to global issues. The images from the Women's Marches, for example, engaged students' visual literacy and digital literacy skills through a critical literacy approach, supporting their development of critical thinking skills and a critical consciousness.

Teachers often face the challenge of both finding and using authentic resources that are developmentally and cognitively appropriate and accessible to students at a particular proficiency level. A rule of thumb with any authentic resource is to change the task, not the text (Glisan & Donato, 2017). If you find a resource that seems important or fits nicely with what you are teaching but you question whether to proceed because the language is beyond your students' proficiency level, develop questions and tasks that allow students to engage with certain aspects of the text at their current proficiency levels. Glisan & Donato (2017) recommend that the authentic resources you choose be *context-appropriate* (in this case, they should have a rich social justice context), *age-appropriate* (the themes and content must be interesting and developmentally appropriate to the learner's age), and *appropriate for the linguistic level of learners* (though the resource may be beyond your students' proficiency level, it should have enough recognizable language for you to design tasks around the resource).

In Novice Level Classrooms

Although it can be more challenging to find the right kind of authentic resource for students of a novice proficiency level, simple Internet searches often yield a variety of resources from which to choose. Below are suggested steps for integrating resources with social justice themes into lessons.

Step 1: Setting the Stage

Returning to the Women's March, a number of images with signs containing various messages could be found. One image had two women holding signs in Spanish and French; the Spanish sign read *Queremos un mundo donde la igualdad sea una realidad, no un objective* ("We want a world where equality is a reality, not an objective"). You can introduce students to the simple, authentic messages and ask them to analyze the image and message and respond to things they notice. It is important to scaffold this process for novice learners by asking questions that help them make sense of the language and the conveyed message. You can encourage students to focus on non-language contextual clues in addition to linguistic aspects. Consider also extracting specific words or chunks of vocabulary from the message for further in-depth exploration.

Step 2: Critical Thinking and Discussion

In this step, ask students to share their initial impressions and interpretations with a partner or small group. Sentence frames can be used to help students engage with each other in the target language (*I see…, I find…most interesting; I am surprised by…*). During this interpersonal task, the pairs or groups decide on a statement they would like to share with the class about their observations or how they interpreted the message and/or image. As a whole class, students can share, and you should encourage students to examine the products, practices and perspectives related to the social justice issue highlighted in the image.

Step 3: Digging Deeper into the Topic

Sometimes, when teaching a current event, you may not want to delve more deeply into it, so stop at Step 2 if you feel that is best. However, if you want to continue to explore the topic with students, extension activities can take place at this point. For example, students could identify meaningful changes that would positively influence the environment of their school and could create their own signs to hang up in the target language, engaging in a presentational task. Another extension activity might be to transition from a global movement like the Women's March to an examination or comparison and contrast of signs from protests in one more target countries to discuss issues that directly affect the people in those countries.

In Intermediate and Advanced Level Classrooms

Students at these levels are able to understand, discuss, and analyze more complex messages. This allows teachers to use authentic resources in different ways, including engagement in civil discourse, an alternative to debate, about the social justice topics raised in the resource.

Step 1: Setting the Stage

After completing an interpretive task that allows the students to engage with the authentic resource and make sense of the message, bring them together to talk explicitly about, and build consensus in, the target language for what "civil discourse" looks and sounds like. This is a by-product of the lesson, but an increasingly important skill for students to engage civically in their communities. A great resource for starting this type of activity is Teaching Tolerance's *Civil Discourse in the Classroom* (2017), which

includes free online materials for great resources for preparing students to use civil discourse in your classroom.

Step 2: Critical Thinking and Discussion

To encourage critical thinking and engage interpersonal communication, use two authentic images and short pieces of written text from Twitter or Instagram that address different viewpoints on a topic. Social media posts can be a great resource for images and short texts that represent varied perspectives in the target language. Students then can respond to the viewpoints as if they were responding on social media, stating respectfully whether they agree or disagree. Encourage students to succinctly rephrase the key argument or point in each message. You can also encourage students to unearth the cultural products, practices or perspectives addressed in the message.

Step 3: Digging Deeper into the Topic

To extend the activities further, students with intermediate and advanced proficiency levels can also learn how civics can be tied to action. For example, we have seen teachers engage students in a service-learning project connected to the topic in which students work directly with members of the target language community in a respectful, responsible way that supports sustained community engagement. Spanish learners could work with a local bilingual elementary school in an afterschool program to co-create short video documentaries in the target language that address issues from the original messages and highlight the richness of their communities. The documentaries could include interviews with community members about their views on current issues that are important to their communities.

Your Turn!

Find an authentic text, image, or another resource related to a social justice topic that can be used in one of your social justice unit lessons. Write a lesson plan that integrates this authentic resource and that uses at least two of the three aforementioned modes of communication (interpretive, interpersonal, presentational). Consider how the text can help you meet your desired lesson and unit objectives.

Conclusion

Over the course of this chapter we have walked you through a process for creating a strong lesson plan that addresses social justice issues. Hopefully by now you have thought through the nuts and bolts of planning and the incorporation of social justice understandings into your daily lessons.

Returning to the beginning of the chapter, Li and his colleagues found great strength, creativity, and support by working together on their planning. Working collaboratively with colleagues creates a space for you to gain access to your colleagues' knowledge, creativity, perspectives, and resources. Collaborative planning and teaching has the potential for positive outcomes for both teachers and students (Thousand, Villa, & Nevin, 2010). Planning can be time-intensive, but entering your classroom with a strong plan will be one of the greatest resources you will use to support your students' development toward your language and social justice objectives.

Discussion Questions

1. Although Li and his colleagues chose a social justice understanding related to identity for their "All About Me" unit, the team could have incorporated others. Think of at least one additional understanding that would be appropriate for this unit for your target language and culture.

2. What would you suggest to a colleague who told you she or he did not believe in writing lesson plans? What arguments could you make in support of planning, particularly for someone just beginning to incorporate social justice into her or his teaching?

3. How might you collaborate with others to address social justice issues into your planning if you were the only world language teacher in your school building? What would collaboration look and sound like in this situation?

4. Think of a time when something you were taught in a world language class was meaningful to you. How did you learn it? Why was it meaningful?

5. Appendix A includes sample activities and resources for various themes. Choose one activity and differentiate it for a class geared toward the novice-mid proficiency level. Then differentiate for intermediate-low students. Finally, differentiate for a group of heritage language learners.

REFERENCES

Clementi, D., & Terrill, L. (2017). *The keys to planning for learning: Effective curriculum, unit, and lesson design* (2nd Ed). Alexandria, VA: American Council of the Teaching of Foreign Languages.

Gaab, C. (2014). *Felipe Alou.* Chandler, AZ: TPRS Publishing, Inc.

Glisan, E. W. & Donato, R. (2017). *Enacting the work of language instruction: High-leverage teaching practices.* Alexandria, VA: The American Council on the Teaching of Foreign Languages.

The National Standards Collaborative Board. (2015). *World-Readiness Standards for Learning Languages.* 4th ed. Alexandria, VA: Author.

Richards, J. C. (1998). What's the use of lesson plans? In J. C. Richards (Ed.), *Beyond training: Perspectives on language teacher education* (pp. 103–121). New York, NY: Cambridge University Press.

Shrum, J., & Glisan, E. W. (2016). *Teacher's handbook: Contextualized language instruction* (5th Ed.) Boston, MA: Heinle.

Teaching Tolerance. (2017). *Civil Discourse in the Classroom.* Retrieved from https://www.tolerance.org/magazine/publications/civil-discourse-in-the-classroom

Thousand, J. S., Villa, R., & Nevin, A. I. (2010). The many faces of collaborative planning and teaching. *Theory Into Practice, 45*(3), 239-248. doi:10.1207/s15430421tip4503_6

CHAPTER 6
Critical Moments

Every teacher has the story of that one moment in the classroom that felt heated, crucial, or somehow critical. Often these moments are outside of the curriculum or the plan, and they require quick thinking and a quick response, sometimes in a way that seems haphazard or confusing. These moments can be instigated by events within your classroom or within school, local, national, or international news. In reflecting on these moments, we often relive and consider what we did, what we could have done, or what we should have done; it replays in our minds, sometimes as a source of regret. In this chapter we will discuss these moments, which we term critical moments, and identify ways to prepare for and respond to them when they occur. We will start the section with some important definitions, then move to some anticipatory and responsive approaches. Finally, we will offer sample scenarios and prompts for you to consider and think through.

A Glimpse into the Classroom

Xin, a native Chinese speaker of Chinese ancestry, is a middle-school teacher for all seventh graders who study Chinese for one term as part of an exploratory language program. He enjoys teaching this age of student because of their energy and curiosity, and he has discovered that teaching language through song can be effective. Xin has written some of his own songs and plays the guitar to lead his students in them.

Before introducing a new song to one of his classes using Total Physical Response, he tells his students to stand up and get ready to learn a new song with the actions. One of his white students, Brandon, loudly announces, "Just a minute, I have to put on my eyes" and proceeds to pull at the corners of his eyes, while the rest of the class begins to laugh. Xin is taken aback and unsure of how to respond. He knows Brandon is joking around, but as a native Chinese speaker Xin feels not only offended but also hurt and embarrassed. He has put a great deal of effort into

engaging his students and thought he was building good relationships with them, and he is surprised that so many of his students find Brandon's antics and statement funny.

Now that you have read this example of a critical moment, please answer these questions:

1. Do you think that Xin should react? If yes, what form should that reaction take? What should he say to Brandon and/or the class?

2. How might this experience be different for Xin than it would be for a Chinese teacher who was not of Chinese ancestry?

3. What could be done to prevent such critical moments in the future in Xin's class?

4. Is there a way to make this into a teachable moment for Xin's students that goes beyond the critical moment itself? How?

Definitions

Critical moments have a number of related names, including *hot moments* (Warren, n.d.) and *kairos moments* (Bartunek & Carboni, 2006). As Warren (n.d.) states, "Hot moments occur when people's feelings—often conflictual—rise to a point that threatens teaching and learning. They can occur during the discussion of issues people feel deeply about, or as a result of classroom dynamics in any field." Relatedly, the kairos moment, as Bartunek and Carboni (2006) emphasize, call for "our best possible response… It is a fundamentally hopeful moment, even if, paradoxically, all seems hopeless" (p. 501). We call these critical moments because we believe this term is most descriptive: these moments are truly critical to maintaining a classroom in which we teach for social justice. Also, the word *critical* echoes the terms *critical pedagogy* and *critical theory*; in this sense, "critical" suggests that we consistently account for the dynamics of power in the classroom and society.

Critical moments can occur when prompted by a number of events in the language classroom, including:

- Unexpected, public comments from students in class;

- Small-group interactions the teacher observes;

- An issue a student brings up in private conversation with the teacher;

- Classroom culture or community issues that develop over time;

- School events that occur outside of the classroom;

- Current events in the local, national, or international news;

- Microaggressions, either observed or reported.

Microaggressions have been defined as "brief, everyday exchanges that send denigrating messages to people of color because they belong to a…minority group…" Perhaps more importantly, they are so "pervasive and automatic in daily conversations and interactions that they are often dismissed and glossed over as being innocent and innocuous" (Sue et al., 2007, p. 273). Sue et al. (2007) were specifically addressing racial microaggressions, although the definition has been since expanded to include other groups. Commonly heard microaggressions might include telling someone who identifies as gay that they are "not like other gay people," or saying to a multiracial individual, "You look exotic. What are you?"[1] Microaggressions can be directed at any member of the classroom community, including the teacher.

Critical Moments and the Use of the Target Language

Critical moments can bring up heated emotions, frustrations, and, importantly, a need for teachers and students to express themselves and to understand one another. However, as world language teachers, we are obligated to use as much of the target language as possible in the classroom and to encourage students to use the language, too. ACTFL has recommended that "language educators and their students use the target language as exclusively as possible (90% plus) at all levels of instruction during

> I have had students who have thought that all Muslims were terrorists. When such comments are brought up, I try to help my students understand why and how someone might become a terrorist, and then we also compare how we have certain communities whom are equally passionate about another cause. Creating empathy or breaking down the stereotype is really important for students."
>
> — Christen Campbell, French teacher, Chapel Hill, North Carolina

instructional time" (ACTFL, 2010). But if students are at a low proficiency level, how can we allow space to address critical moments adequately while still using the target language in the classroom?

The use of the target language in addressing a critical moment depends on the students' proficiency level. If they are at an intermediate-high or higher proficiency in the target language, they will likely possess the language skills to address the moment in the classroom without using English. Even so, you might consider allowing students to reflect on the moment in English outside of class in a journal or a vlog, or to meet outside of class time. For lower-proficiency students, you may have to plan more strategically. The *NCSSFL-ACTFL Intercultural Reflection Tool* (2017) suggests the following structure as a framework for reflective activities:

1. an introductory in-class component in the target language;

2. a deeper reflection outside of class in English, or, if the learner's proficiency level allows, in the target language; and

3. a follow-up in-class target language component (NCSSFL-ACTFL, 2017, p. 1).

---

[1] Further examples can be seen on the website microaggressions.com.

This structure might work in some cases, particularly in those of older students with lower proficiency levels. In some cases, authentic or adapted materials in the target language can offer the students an important tool to mediate their learning. (More suggestions about target language materials will be addressed later in this chapter.) Offering students the opportunity to address a moment both in the target language and in English can be a very successful technique.

Sometimes it might be preferable to address the critical moment completely in English. Perhaps the moment can be seen as a part of the 10% of the weekly instructional time spent in English. Alternately, you could shift the priority in the case of this important teachable moment, but be sure not to privilege English and subtly indicate to your students that English is used when things are important, and that the target language is for everything else. If the switch to English only is noticeable in your classroom, it is worth explaining that you are doing this solely because you believe every student needs to understand and express themselves in their first language for the purposes of this discussion. This is a decision that you, as the teacher, have to make as it best suits you.

Anticipating a Critical Moment

Hill (2017) has suggested that teachers can prepare for and prevent a critical moment and organize responses after it has occurred. Anticipatory approaches include many of the community-building techniques we have outlined in Chapter 2. Hill further advocates the establishment of community guidelines and discussion norms that anticipate the possibility of critical moments: "Developing community in a classroom reduces anonymity, promotes civility, fosters accountability, demonstrates conscious inclusivity, and creates a welcoming and inclusive environment where the discomfort of learning can happen" (Hill, 2017, p. 2). This can be achieved by questioning students about their experiences with critical moments with such questions as:

- What makes you comfortable in a class discussion?

- What conditions help you to learn the best?

- Have you ever had a time when you have been uncomfortable in a class? When? What could have helped to make that better?

These questions could be asked individually, by having students write their answers on an index card, or collectively, in a class discussion. As the use of the target language is always at the forefront of the world language teacher's mind, you should either save this discussion for the small amount of time you teach in English or, with an upper-level class, provide them with appropriate supports to discuss it in the target language. The students' responses can and should be used as the basis for discussion norms for the class.

Another form of anticipatory preparation is your own preparation as a teacher. Part of addressing critical moments relates to your own comfort and ease in addressing such complex topics as race, class, sexual orientation, disability, and controversial events in the news. The *Teaching Tolerance* website includes several resources designed to help teachers self-assess their own vulnerabilities, strengths, and needs in addressing these topics (*Let's Talk*, 2017). Other ways to self-assess could include rating your comfort level in talking about racism, classism, or sexism (noting that your comfort level in each of these areas will probably be different), then finishing the sentence: "The hard part about talking about [topic] is…." and "The most beneficial part about talking about [topic] is…" (*Let's Talk*, 2017, p. 4). It is also important to reflect on conversations you have had in the past about these topics with people who are both like you and unlike you.

These self-assessments can help you focus on your strengths and encourage you to seek out further training or readings that address your weaknesses. They can also help you reflect on training and advice you have received in the past and imagine how you might apply it to future critical moments. You can find resources to help you within and outside of your school. Finally, when a critical moment does occur, you will be able to more easily access your own emotions and thoughts on the topic from having done that background reflection.

No matter how much you may have anticipated critical moments in your own classroom community-building, reflection and self-assessment, critical moments are not totally preventable. The complexity of the classroom, the young people you work with, and the world surrounding you can all contribute to critical moments and are variables you cannot control. Above all, a critical moment is not a failure, but an opportunity.

Responding to a Critical Moment

Responding to a critical moment can take many different forms. Perhaps the first thing to examine is how ready you are to respond immediately to a critical moment. Are you calm? Do you see a path forward? Can you control your emotions as you respond? This is particularly important when the critical moment involves or affects you personally or acutely, as it did for Xin in the vignette at the start of the chapter. It is also important if the critical moment visibly upsets or disturbs other students. You should never feel as if you are forcing yourself or your students to respond to a critical moment before you are ready. Furthermore, if you, as the teacher, present distress or strong emotions of anger or sadness to your students as you respond, that is often what they will react to and remember, not the words you are saying or what you are trying to teach to them. As Warren (2006) suggested, you should think about leaving the dance floor of the class discussion and going up to the balcony. This means you should move yourself to a figurative location where you can be at a reasonable distance from the discussion and from your emotions. If you cannot do this at least in part, and if you feel that other students cannot move beyond their own strong emotions to have a productive discussion, then you should reconsider an immediate reaction.

At this point, if you do not feel ready to respond, a simple statement can pause the class for a moment until you feel calm and reasonably comfortable in formulating your response. Examples might include:

- "This is not the place for statements like that."

- "I want to acknowledge what is in the news, but I'm not ready to talk about it today."

- "I'm going to give you a minute to think about what you said."

- "That's not how we talk here" or "That's not what we do here."

- "I'm not ready to respond to that, but it does need a response."

These statements could be followed with something like, "We're going to move on for now, but I will want to talk about this again in the future." This immediate response should not indicate a need for your students to respond at that moment; that is, it should not be formulated as a question or a prompt for a discussion. Your students must also be given a chance to respond and interact in the future, when you take up the critical moment again. If you never address the moment again, you risk indicating tacit approval and allowing it to be an acceptable part of your class. This action will give you time to gather your thoughts and calm yourself down. Not that your own feelings cannot be expressed, but they must be formulated carefully so your students can hear and understand them.

When you are ready, you should respond to the critical moment. Recall that it is good to be in the balcony of the class at this point, stepping back from and out of the critical moment and considering it as something to be explored. At this point, we will consider two main types of critical moments separately, as their differences will dictate how you should consider proceeding. First, we will examine moments that arise in the classroom spontaneously, due to the actions or words of students in the class. Then we will look at critical moments prompted by events in the news.

Student-Prompted Critical Moments

When a student says or does something that prompts a critical moment, first **listen for the subtext** of what the speakers/instigators are saying, rather than the words themselves. For instance, the use of a slur is not about the slur itself as a forbidden word, but about disrespecting the group the slur targets. Some critical moments might stem from fundamental misunderstandings about the target culture or a lack of knowledge about a group of people.

Use of a slur might also be the product of an implicit or unconscious bias (Moule, 2009), wherein the student is drawing from years of socialization about race, gender, and other forms of difference. In the case of unconscious bias, the speakers/instigators would never consider themselves racist or homophobic but might make simple, unconscious associations that would create a critical moment when expressed in specific circumstances. Consider this as you formulate your response, rather than reacting solely to the spoken words. Additionally, in reacting, try to **maintain a relationship with the speaker/instigator,** remembering the authority and power we, as teachers, hold in the classroom and over our students. Your focus should be on the critical moments, not the speakers/instigators. Hold solely their words or actions up for examination, not them personally (Hill, 2017; Teaching Tolerance, n.d.).

As you move to take action, consider who needs to be addressed. Some critical moments might be better addressed individually with the speaker/instigator or in a small group, particularly when the critical moment did not occur with the whole class as a witness.

As a first action, **repeat back what you heard or observed from the speaker/instigator** (Teaching Tolerance, n.d.). By doing so, you can verify that you did indeed hear or observe correctly. You can also draw the speaker/instigator's attention to her or his words or actions. After doing this, you can **open up the conversation** by asking general questions of the individual, including:

- What do you mean by that?

- How did you get there?

- If that's what you say, then what are the implications?

As you are doing this, continue to maintain your focus on what was said or done, not the speaker/instigator. Try to get the speaker/instigator to express or acknowledge the subtext of the comments, and to draw a line between the critical moment and larger statements about the community of the classroom and the school.

Depending on the developmental level of your students and the nature of the critical moment, you can also ask

other members of the class if they have a response or a thought about what was said. Remind students that, although they are welcome to express emotions, the class must still be productive and respectful, and that everyone in the class has a responsibility to the others. This is a difficult and perhaps controversial thought in the face of truly offensive critical moments, but the focus needs to be on developing and moving forward as a class and community. Some possible prompts for other students in the class could be:

- What did you feel when you heard/observed this?

- What would you like to say in response?

- How do you think we can move forward as a class from this?

Students can also journal or write about the critical moments to answer these questions. This option can permit students who would not speak up in a large class discussion to express themselves to you. It can also allow students to express anger or pain about the critical moment, when they might not feel comfortable doing so in the large class discussion. You can also talk with individual students outside of class (either the speaker/instigator, or bystanding students) to follow up with them and let them express themselves more personally to you. This action would be appropriate in the rare cases when you have an intentional provocateur who actively wishes to disrupt the class by creating critical moments. In that case, treat the moment as a student conduct issue, following appropriate disciplinary procedures for your school or institution.

Critical Moments from Outside of the Classroom

When a critical moment is prompted by events outside of the classroom, the teacher faces more choices as well as more pressures. These moments could include a graffiti incident involving slurs at your school, a prominent Supreme Court or other national policy decision, a natural disaster, or a terrorist attack. Because this type of critical moment is not an immediate moment in the classroom, you can choose not to address it at all. Furthermore, you might face pressure from administration or colleagues to not mention something. A recent example from a school district we know occurred after the United States presidential election of 2016, when all teachers in a high school were emailed before school the day after the election to tell them not to discuss it with their students.

Indeed, teachers have several options when considering how to address a critical moment brought up by current events. The options include:

1. Do not bring the critical moment into class at all. Beyond administrative pressure, this can also be due to discomfort or lack of experience with the topic.

2. Contextualize the critical moment within the international community (in the case of moments based in broader current events). Instead of focusing on processing the moment, look at students' reactions and parallel experiences in the target culture(s).

3. Share your personal views and experiences. Some critical moments might lend themselves more readily to sharing your own experiences, particularly if they involve a location or a community you know well.

4. Be a facilitator for student discussion. Offer space in your classroom for students to process the event through careful prompts and activities designed to get them to process the event.

5. Offer a combination of the options mentioned in options 2-4 above.

Your choice of option will depend on your own level of comfort and experience, as well as your background and your knowledge of the event itself. We recommend looking at the resources on the Teaching Tolerance website, particularly their publications, including a useful magazine issue from 2016 about how to lead a discussion on the United States presidential election (https://www.tolerance.org/magazine/fall-2016). That issue includes important tips for addressing political differences within one classroom.

If you do decide to address the current event as a critical moment in your world language classroom, consider how you will use the target language and culture(s). Unlike other forms of critical moments, this one can allow for

preparation and planning, albeit in a short timeline. To address these moments, consider **authentic materials** as vital resources. Teachers often face the challenge of both finding and using authentic resources that are developmentally and cognitively appropriate and accessible to students at a particular proficiency level; finding appropriate materials for novice-level students can be particularly challenging. However, the Internet and social media give us access to a wide variety of images, media-based photos, videos, audio, and other resources with rich social justice themes appropriate for a range of ages and proficiency levels. These materials could include photographs or timelines from publications from the target culture(s). Students at lower proficiencies could look at captions and titles to examine the resources.

In addition, you can hone students' **visual literacy skills,** in which students are asked to make sense of what they see and justify their answers. For example, if your school has been dealing with bullying, you can find a picture from an anti-bullying campaign in the target culture. Students can be asked questions like "What do you see? What do you think? What do you wonder?" or they can be asked to step inside a character in the picture and narrate it from a first person perspective. For more advanced students, you could include texts including editorials and reports on the current event, and students can participate in more complex tasks such as summarizing perspectives and giving their own opinions on the topic. Recall also that, if the event occurred in the United States, other locations in the world will have reactions and responses to the event, and looking at those authentic materials will be important openings for your students.

Developing Curriculum Based on Critical Moments

Depending on your flexibility with the curriculum, these critical moments can inspire the creation of a new, original unit that will allow you and your students to explore the topic in depth, particularly in contexts where the critical moment can be connected closely with something that occurs in the target culture or using the target language. Here are some specific steps you can take to engage students of different proficiency levels.

Step 1: Setting the Stage

Teaching a unit about a critical moment must first begin with a close examination of the moment so students feel sufficiently informed to build on their knowledge. For instance, images of signs from the worldwide Women's Marches of January 2017 were readily available on social media and in the news. The signs' messages revealed a multitude of cultural practices and perspectives about human rights, social justice, peace, democracy, equity, and other issues related to civic engagement. Moreover, these signs held clear connections to global issues. For instance, in one demonstration, a Spanish sign read *Queremos un mundo donde la igualdad sea una realidad, no un objectivo* ("We want a world where equality is a reality, not an objective").

One way to teach about these movements with novice-level learners would be to ask students to examine the images carefully and point to things they notice. You could scaffold the students' learning with sentence frames ("I see…," "I find…," "I am surprised by…") and asking questions that help students make sense of the language and message conveyed. You could also extract specific words or chunks of vocabulary from the message to emphasize specialized terminology that reveals important perspectives from the participants.

In **intermediate or advanced** proficiency level classes you could use two authentic images from the marches or short pieces of written text from Twitter or Instagram posts that address different viewpoints on the marches. You could then ask your students to succinctly rephrase each message's key argument or point and explain how they are the same and different. Additionally, you could explicitly ask students to connect cultural practices to perspectives by having them connect the images or posts with larger policies and beliefs in different subgroups in the target culture(s).

Step 2: Critical Thinking and Discussion

Students can be encouraged to build on the information they were given in Step 1 to develop their own arguments and thoughts about the critical moment. You could start by asking them to share their initial impressions and interpretations with a partner or small group. At the **novice** level, you could teach gambits ("I agree with you," "I have a different opinion") that learners can use with each other as they engage in the conversation with partners or groups. During this interpersonal task, the pairs or groups could decide on a statement they would like to share with the class about their observations or how they interpreted the message and/or image.

At the **intermediate or advanced** levels, students could respond to the viewpoints as if they were responding on social media, for example, stating respectfully whether they agree or disagree. They could elect to present their opinions from their own cultural perspective(s), or they could role-play in their responses as if they were members of one of the target cultures. You could also bring the students together to build consensus in the target language for what civil discourse looks and sounds like. This is a byproduct of the lesson, but an increasingly important skill for students to engage civically in their communities (see also Shuster, 2017).

Step 3: Moving to Action

When possible, we recommend finding ways to move to action on a topic, going beyond in-class discussions into promoting social change. For example, students could identify meaningful changes that would positively influence their school's environment and could create their own signs to hang up in the target language, thus perform a presentational task. You could engage students in a service-learning project connected to the topic in which students work directly with members of the target language community in a respectful, responsible way that supports sustained community engagement. Spanish learners could work with a local bilingual elementary school in an after-school program to co-create short video documentaries in the target language that address issues from the original messages and highlight the richness of their communities. The documentaries could include interviews with community members about their views on current issues that are important to their communities.

Your Turn!

Find an authentic image or another resource related to a social justice topic that would be an important critical moment to address in a lesson. Develop a lesson around this authentic image.

Following Up on a Critical Moment

After a critical moment occurs and you have responded, consider how you will move forward in the class, and build on the interactions that resulted from that critical moment. Lessons learned from the critical moments can sometimes be formalized in class guidelines about interactions or civil discourse. For instance, a new class guideline might be established that discourages the use of slurs or statements that generalize about one group and that invites students to respectfully challenge one another when a slur is used. In other circumstances, reference the discussion that took place after the critical moment when class interactions appear heated or disrespectful. For instance: "Okay, everyone, remember that sometimes what we say is not what other people might hear—be clear with your words and respectful in your tone!" Critical moments from outside of the classroom can be brought up as new discussions begin later in the year. For example: "Before we talk about this free speech debate in [target country], let's put up on the board some of the things we remember about the free speech debate we discussed a few weeks ago." Critical moments can also represent important moments of community-building in the classroom; if a shared understanding has been reached, asking students to recall that moment can be powerful.

Sample Critical Moments

In each example below, we explain a critical moment from our own experience or that of one of our teacher colleagues. We then explain some possible responses. (Note: The descriptions of some of these critical moments can be difficult to read. Additionally, the responses might not work in your context or with your own personality. We hope they can illustrate the forms responses can take.)

Scenario A

The French teacher is teaching her sixth graders a French playground dance and rhyme that requires them to haphazardly pair off. One male student, upon discovering that sometimes in the dance his partner would be another male, shouts, "I don't want to be *gay!*"

Possible Response to Scenario A: The teacher responds by pausing the instructions and repeating the words back to the student, "You said, 'I don't want to be gay'?" The student acknowledges that he did say that, and explains, "I think that dancing with a boy is sort of gay, and I don't want to do it." The teacher begins the discussion by stating that the activity is not meant to pair students up romantically, and that many dances in many cultures are not female-male in organization. She asks, "Can anyone think of dances that might have women dancing with women or men dancing with men?" The students come up with ballet, and, with some prompting, even dances at their school where groups of same-sex friends dance together. The teacher then states that the student's statement about "not wanting to be gay" could indicate that being LGBTQ is allegedly bad or undesirable. The teacher says that the speaker certainly has a right not to identify as LGBTQ but needs to express himself with more acceptance and thoughtfulness in her class.

Scenario B

A male teacher, originally from Peru, teaches Spanish in an area with a strong Spanish-speaking community. One morning early in the semester of a Spanish I class at a high school, one of his ninth graders, who is white, announces that her parents employ Spanish speakers and that she is learning Spanish so she, too, can be the "boss" of Spanish-speaking employees.

Possible Response to Scenario B: Because of the teacher's own background, the student's statement immediately bothers him. Instead of responding right away, he says, "I'd like for you to think about what you said a little more. We're going to talk about it later this week." Then, after reflecting, consulting with colleagues, and gathering his thoughts, he brings the topic back to the class in a discussion of reasons for learning a new language. First he repeats back the original student's comment and asks if he understood it correctly, and then he asks the class if they would like to express agreement or disagreement with that statement. Some students agree with the original speaker, saying that knowing Spanish is important for talking with people in the workplace, especially in the restaurant or agriculture industries. Upon the teacher's prompting, students start to think through where Spanish-speakers work in the United States and why, and what jobs might require a knowledge of Spanish. The teacher also asks students to consider the roles of power and privilege in business, as fewer minoritized individuals are in management roles. He supplements this discussion with evidence from employment data from the government. The students develop a more complex understanding of the nature of working in jobs where Spanish is spoken.

Scenario C

Students in a university-level Arabic class are angry about gun violence in the United States, particularly incidents that have taken place in schools. After another recent gun violence event in the news, the students are talking about it in class and draw the Arabic instructor into the conversation. They wonder why this is so prevalent in the U.S. and discuss participation in a local protest and march scheduled for the next day. The instructor can see that the conversation about recent events in the news is beginning to move the students away from the curriculum topics, but she does not want to discourage the students from discussing this issue.

Possible Response to Scenario C: The instructor refocuses the students, acknowledging that their conversation is very important and that, as young people, they are in a great position to use their voices and take action by participating in a protest if they decide they would like to do so. She decides that, because of their interest in the topic, it would be a good opportunity to explore it from the perspectives of various Arabic-speaking countries. So she promises the class that she will return to the topic with them but says she needs some time to prepare for it so they can engage meaningfully and effectively with each other. She explains that she would like to contextualize this topic within Arabic-speaking communities and be able to compare and contrast that with a United States

context for the topic. The teacher moves on to other topics that day in class.

However, outside of class, she compiles authentic texts in the form of images, social media posts, and short news articles from various Arabic-speaking countries about their reactions to gun violence in the U.S. She looks for different stances and opinions within the international community and develops a few lesson plans around gun laws and gun violence in Arabic-speaking countries that will take place the next week at the end of the current unit. She plans for the students to begin by engaging in visual literacy activities around some of the images she found, then to participate in an interpretive task via a WebQuest to read the social media posts and articles that show reactions to recent events in the U.S. In class, she plans to engage students in civil discourse, discuss, compare and contrast perspectives, and debate about the topic from various viewpoints. She hopes these lesson plans will both address recent events and enable the students to articulate their own perspectives and gain an understanding of perspectives of Arabic speakers in various communities.

Scenario D

Just before class starts, a high-school teacher of Japanese overhears two students talking loudly about the body odor of one of the school's newly arrived refugees. They express disgust and laugh loudly as they speculate that the student "probably doesn't know what soap and deodorant are."

Possible Response to Scenario D: Because this happens before the class begins, the teacher is uncertain if she should address it at that moment or wait until later. She decides to address it after class and individually so the two instigators do not feel attacked or defensive in being called out publicly about what they might have assumed was a private conversation. When they stay to talk with her after class at her request, she repeats back to them what she heard. She asks them if they have anything they would like to say about their choice to make those statements. The students say, "We were just kidding around—we wouldn't say it to their faces!" and "We weren't talking to you!" She listens to them and acknowledges that they were surprised at being overheard in this way. She also explains that school is a public space and they were talking loudly right in front of her and many other students.

Using a story from her own time studying abroad in Japan, the teacher then illustrates how cultural differences can extend to differences in hygiene practices. She also asks them to think about what it means to be part of a community in the school and how they can be more welcoming in word and deed. To follow up, the teacher talks with the refugee liaison in the school and explains that this might be a cultural component the refugee students might want to know. She does not address it with the class as a whole.

Discussion Questions

1. What types of critical moments do you believe you would feel comfortable addressing in your classroom? What types of moments would be particularly difficult for you?

2. Many teachers have an example of a critical moment that occurred in their teaching, or, alternately, they witnessed one as a student or heard about one from a colleague. Think about an example of a critical moment you know about. How did the teacher react? Following the tips in this chapter, how could you imagine a different reaction?

3. How do you think you will use the target language in the context of a critical moment in the classroom?

4. What are some alternate responses to the scenarios provided at the end of the chapter that you would consider using?

REFERENCES

American Council on the Teaching of Foreign Languages. (2010). *Position Statement on Use of the Target Language in the Classroom.* Retrieved from https://www.actfl.org/news/position-statements/use-the-target-language-the-classroom

Bartunek, J. M., & Carboni, I. (2006). A time for hope: A response to Nancy Adler. *Academy of Management Learning and Education, 5,* 500-504.

Bell, M., & Lindberg, M. (2017). *Let's talk: Discussing race, racism, and other difficult topics with students.* (2017). Montgomery, AL: Teaching Tolerance, A Project of the Southern Poverty Law Center. Retrieved from https://www.tolerance.org/sites/default/files/2017-09/TT-Lets%20Talk-2017%20Final.pdf

Hill, S. E. (2017, May). *Dealing with racist—and other inappropriate—moments in the classroom.* Paper presented at Wakonse Conference on College Teaching, Shelby, MI.

Moule, J. (2009). Understanding unconscious bias and unintentional racism. *Phi Delta Kappan, 90*(5), 320-326. Retrieved from http://journals.sagepub.com/doi/pdf/10.1177/003172170909000504

National Council of State Supervisors for Languages and American Council on the Teaching of Foreign Languages. (2017). *Reflection: Intercultural Communication. NCSSFL-ACTFL Intercultural Reflection Tool.* Retrieved from https://www.actfl.org/sites/default/files/CanDos/Intercultural%20Can-Dos_Reflections%20Scenarios.pdf

Shuster, K. (2017). *Civil Discourse in the Classroom.* Retrieved from https://www.tolerance.org/sites/default/files/2017-10/Civil-Discourse-v2-CoverRedesign-Oct2017.pdf

Sue, D. W., Capodilupo, C. M., Torino, G. C., Bucceri, J. M., Holder, A., Nadal, K. L., & Esquilin, M. (2007). Racial microaggressions in everyday life: implications for clinical practice. *American Psychologist, 62*(4), 271.

Warren, L. (n.d.). Managing hot moments in the classroom. *The Derek Bok Center for Teaching and Learning, Harvard University.* Retrieved from https://bokcenter.harvard.edu/hot-moments

CHAPTER 7

Self-Assessment and Reflection

Assessment has been addressed as an important part of the process of planning lessons for social justice throughout the first chapters of this book. Formal assessment, both formative and summative, should not be isolated from lesson planning and classroom procedures. However, some forms of assessment can be combined with or incorporated into reflective practice, both for the students and for you as the teacher. These reflective assessments might come after the unit or project is finished, or they might be incorporated throughout the unit. This chapter will focus on how to make room for reflection for everyone in your classroom.

A Glimpse into the Classroom

Carol and Oscar both teach Spanish at the same high school in an urban district; they share the responsibilities for teaching the beginning two levels of the Spanish courses. Because they work together closely, they have developed the same social justice unit to teach their novice-mid/novice-high students. This unit involves a service-learning project with a local community center where immigrants from Spanish-speaking countries take citizenship classes. Because they are evening classes, the citizens-to-be are encouraged to bring their children, all of whom are emergent bilinguals. Carol and Oscar's high school students work with these children during their parents' classes.

This year, partly in response to reduced funding for arts education in local public schools, Carol and Oscar have developed a project to work with the children and enlisted a bilingual art educator to create a mural in the community center. The theme is citizenship, and Carol and Oscar's students must lead the young children through generating ideas, planning, and then creating the mural. Their intention is for the teenagers to get to know the children, use their Spanish, and help the children to understand what their parents or guardians are doing in seeking citizenship. Carol and Oscar's students also examine the children's perspectives on citizenship in general, and compare and

contrast it with their own perspectives. Because reflection is an important part of any service-learning project, particularly one as potentially challenging as this, Carol and Oscar prioritize student reflection by tying it into assessment. They also incorporate extensive teacher reflection into the unit. They decide, however, to accomplish this in two different ways.

Carol uses a journal system, where students write weekly about their reactions to what they learn. They are allowed to write in English, but the prompts are given in Spanish, and they are encouraged to write the first few sentences of their introduction in Spanish. Carol has given them a long list of sample sentences to help with the Spanish writing. Prompts include:

- Explain your feelings about working with your students this week.

- What was challenging, and what was easy, about working with the students this week?

- What did you learn this week that you did not know before?

- What would you change if you were to redo this week's work?

Carol responds to each entry with holistic comments in Spanish. When strong emotions or issues arise in the journal entries, she meets with students individually during quiet work time or study periods. The journal entries are assessed at the end of the unit based on completion and the accurate and appropriate use of Spanish in the introductory sentences.

During this time, Carol completes her own journal entries in Spanish, responding to the same prompts while reflecting on the students' learning and her own teaching. She shares selected portions of her responses with her students in Spanish and English during regular debriefing conversations, allowing them to understand her reactions to the class activities as well as her interpretation of how they are learning. Later, she will use these journal entries as evidence of reflective practice for her end-of-year self-evaluation and her teaching portfolio.

Oscar guides students through reflection and self-assessment with the help of a set of questionnaires and rubrics the students complete at the end of the unit, beginning with a self-assessment questionnaire he has created using Google forms. In this questionnaire, the students first assess in Spanish if they have met the service-learning project's objectives that week. Then they are provided with space to write in English or Spanish about what they have learned, their favorite and least favorite moments in the lesson, and what they still wish to learn or do. Oscar reviews these and calculates grades based on his understanding of how honest the students are in their self-assessments based on their performances in the final task. The highest grade a student can earn if writing only in English is B+; at least half of the open-ended questions must be answered in Spanish to receive an A or A–. The self-assessments are included as a minor part of the overall unit grade.

The students also complete a peer assessment wherein each observes another student's teaching and read that student's lesson plans. They are then assigned other students to assess randomly. On this peer assessment, in Spanish, they fill out a checklist that covers the required elements of the assignment, marking how well the other students have fulfilled the requirements. Then they are given a space to offer narrative comments about the strengths and weaknesses of the lesson. They are not to sign their names to the peer assessment form. Oscar collects all peer assessments, checks them for accuracy and appropriateness, and then redistributes them to the assessed students when he hands out final grades.

At the end of the project, Oscar reflects on his teaching and the students' learning, in two ways: (1) He fills out the same form the students use for their self-assessment, examining whether he has met his instructional goals, and then writes narrative comments that summarize his experience. (2) He uses the district's performance evaluation system criteria to rate his own instruction.

To think through the above vignettes, please answer these questions:

1. Does one of the approaches to reflection appeal to you more than the other? Why?

2. What do you think of the teachers' use of the target language (Spanish) in the student reflections and assessments? Would you make any changes for your own students?

Encouraging Self-Assessment and Reflection in Students

Key elements of social justice education are reflection and self-assessment (Hackman, 2005) and the cultivation of students who are capable of critical thinking. The latter involves more than just meeting specific social justice objectives in a unit's framework. Teachers must also offer students opportunities for reflection and self-assessment, for they empower students by giving them responsibility for evaluating their own progress (see also Shrum & Glisan, 2016) and encouraging them to question the bigger picture of how their perspective on social justice affects their work (Osborn, 2006). In this section, we will describe a few ways to encourage students to self-assess and reflect, including self-assessment, peer assessment, portfolio and journaling activities.

All approaches this chapter describes are offered as if they would occur in English. We do not recommend this in classes for higher-proficiency students, who are presumed to be at an intermediate-low level or higher and would be capable of self-assessment in the target language. Forced-choice items, where students must only read and select from a limited number of options, can be easily offered in the target language at lower levels. However, students at lower language-proficiency levels should not be expected to self-assess in longer written responses in the target language; that would greatly impede their ability to truly express themselves in the depth the task would require.

Self-Assessment Questionnaires

Self-assessment can be a powerful way to stimulate students to reflect on their capacities in the language. One powerful framework for this type of self-assessment can be found in the *NCSSFL-ACTFL Can-Do Statements*

(NCSSFL-ACTFL, 2017), which help students identify what they can do with the language, both before a segment of instruction as a way to set goals, and after instruction as a way to self-assess and set new goals. For instance, a Can-Do Statement at the Advanced-Low level of Interpersonal Communication reads: "I can maintain conversations by providing explanations and comparisons of preferences, opinions, and advice on familiar and concrete academic and social topics using a few simple paragraphs across major time frames" (NCSSFL-ACTFL, 2017, p. 13).

A student self-assessment questionnaire about a social justice lesson or unit can first include Can-Do Statements performance indicators. You can also create similar **forced-choice items** that relate directly to the lesson's social justice objectives. To create those items related to your social justice objectives, ask yourself:

- What are the main social justice objectives of the lesson or unit?

- How can you adapt these objectives into questions students can answer?

You certainly can directly ask students if they have met an objective. For example:

1. I can describe how socioeconomic status influences French speakers' ability to maintain healthy lifestyles.	Yes	With Help	Not Yet

Indirect prompts can also be used:

- If I had to explain [insert concept] to a friend who doesn't take this class, I'd know what to say.

- I can report on what I learned about [insert concept here] in this unit.

Questions should be worded in ways appropriate to the students' developmental and knowledge levels. For instance, in the question above, if the students had not been explicitly introduced to the concept of "socioeconomic status," words more appropriate (in the target language or in English) should be used. The meaning of the self-assessment questions should be self-evident to the students

taking it, assuming that they have been attending class and completing their work adequately.

Younger learners and learners at novice levels of proficiency can benefit from the use of visual or graphic representations when evaluating their progress. Visuals, images, or emojis can be used in the performance statements or in the evaluation levels.

I can give examples of prejudice words and pictures. (Teaching Tolerance Standards, Justice 12)	😀	😐	🙁
I can recognize that words, behaviors, rules, and laws that treat people unfairly based on their group identities cause real harm. (Teaching Tolerance Standards, Justice 13)	😀	😐	🙁
I can understand that life is easier for some people and harder for others based on who they are and where they were born. (Tolerance Standards, Justice 14)	😀	😐	🙁

The second type of question to include in this self-assessment questionnaire is an **open-ended question,** which enables the students to write more about their thoughts. Good prompts include:

- What was the most interesting area for you in this unit?

- What was the most difficult thing for you in this unit?

- What surprised you the most about this unit, and why?

- What grade do you think you received on your work, and why?

- What did you learn in this unit that changed or questioned your thinking?

- How could you take action in response to something you learned in this unit?

Responses to these questions, beyond simply encouraging active reflection, offer you an important snapshot of your students' experiences, which can later be used to revise and improve social justice instruction.

We suggest that your students complete this self-assessment after a unit is completed, preferably within a day or two of the final assignment. However, as with the *NCSSFL-ACTFL Can-Do Statements* (NCSSFL-ACTFL, 2017), students may use versions of these questionnaires to set goals be-fore a new unit. To do this, you will simply change the wording of the items to be appropriate for students who have not yet completed the unit of study. For a unit that is less identifiable and bounded, this type of self-assessment questionnaire might not be appropriate; see the next sections for ways to encourage student reflection in those contexts.

Write a self-assessment questionnaire with at least five items for the unit you developed as a result of work in Chapter 3 or 4.

Peer Assessment

Peer assessment can take a variety of forms and serve a variety of functions, some more conducive to reflection, others simply enhancing a more formal grading procedure on the instructor's part. Since each form of peer assessment empowers students to consider their learning from a different perspective, we recommend you adopt at least one as a part of a summative assessment of social justice instruction when possible and inform students that they will be asked to conduct peer assessments (and have their own work submitted to a peer assessment) at the start of the unit. This can enhance students' feelings about their accountability to their peers and the classroom community.

Three forms of peer assessment can be particularly useful in examining social justice learning in the world language classroom:

1. **Standard assessment checklist.** This type of peer assessment requires students to read, watch, or examine another student's work, and to identify whether important components (e.g., five sentences in the target language, six slides with illustrations, ten minutes of the presentation) are present or absent. This is one of the more typical forms of peer assessment. It requires a minimum amount of reflection, although it does encourage students to look at one another's work in some detail.

2. **Quality assessment worksheet.** This type of peer assessment more closely mimics the self-assessment described above. It encourages peers to look at one another's work and see if it meets the unit objectives. Items similar to those in the self-assessment questionnaire could be used, with the open-ended questions shifted slightly to encourage each student to respond to another's work.

3. **Group work assessment.** Since the units and projects this book describes might be assigned to groups or pairs rather than individual students, we recommend that teachers include a group-work assessment as a part of the peer assessment process. This assessment should be equal parts reflection and report, asking students to discuss their own roles in the group as well as their assessments of their peers in the group. Open-ended questions are often very effective in this case. They can ask students to report or reflect on topics such as:

- the contributions made by each group member;

- the roles adopted by each group member;

- the ways in which the group members made decisions about sharing the work; or

- the perspectives (differing or the same) adopted by the group members.

Write a set of at least five items or questions that can be used to guide peer assessment in a way appropriate for the unit you created in Chapter 3 or 4.

Portfolios

This book primarily describes a unit-oriented way of organizing social justice instruction in the world language classroom. That is, we have described instruction in social justice education in terms of unified, coherent lessons that work together to create a unit, often resulting in a final product that is assessed in a summative way. However, social justice lessons and units can also contribute to content in a larger portfolio that encompasses other parts of classroom instruction.

A portfolio is a collection of evidence in the form of **artifacts** that illustrate a student's knowledge of content, use of strategies, and/or attitudes about the classroom (Shrum & Glisan, 2010; Byram, 2000). Artifacts can include anything a student produces, from worksheets to videos to journal entries. Beyond selecting artifacts for the portfolio, students also customarily write self-reflections in which they describe why they included the artifact and how it reflects their knowledge.

Much has been written about the use of portfolios in world language education. They have shown great utility in assessing students' knowledge of culture, communicative competence, and intercultural competence (see Byram's work, including Byram, 1997, 2000, for more information on this topic), thus dovetail nicely with a social justice approach to world languages instruction.

To include students' learning about social justice in a class portfolio, we recommend you follow the steps you would follow to establish criteria for any other portfolio artifacts (see Shrum & Glisan, 2016). The portfolio's general guidelines, structure, organization and logistics should already be determined and clearly stated to the students. Then identify the social justice objectives—those you had determined when planning your unit—that students would need to address with their portfolio artifacts.

Next, provide tasks to help students obtain their portfolio artifacts, and give guidelines for the students' self-reflections on the artifacts. Formative assessment tasks, as described in Chapter 5, can be excellent sources of portfolio artifacts. The students' self-reflections about the social justice-related artifacts should follow a similar structure to what was described in the self-assessment open-ended questions above. Depending on the prominence of portfolios in your assessment procedures, the social justice portfolio artifacts can be included as major or minor components.

Journaling

Student journaling can offer a consistent, informal format for student reflection. Journaling involves a repeated process of language production that includes reflection on the student's learning experiences, either in written form, such as diaries or blogs, or in spoken form, through video blogging or podcasting. Journaling can be assigned according to a prompt or sentence-starter, or a more general prompt might be repeated across entries. Journal prompts could include:

- What did you learn this week that you didn't know before?

- Put yourself in the position of [...]. How would you react?

- Explain your feelings about the reading/video.

- Have you ever been in [...] situation? Tell that story, and explain what you did.

- Who do you agree with in the debate? Why?

Journal assignments should be frequent, and requirements clearly defined. When the target language is encouraged, the students should be informed explicitly about the expectations in terms of accuracy; usually the journals should be ungraded and uncorrected to emphasize the importance of the content. Feedback should be given, but it should focus on the content rather than grammar correction. If a grade must be given, we recommend a summative grade at the end of the series of entries, focusing on completion and target language use, rather than an individual grade for each entry.

Due to the increasing availability of technology in the world language classroom, we encourage you to consider its use in journaling assignments. Besides allowing students to write all journal entries online as blogs, you can encourage them to create video blog (vlog) entries or record podcasts.

Your Turn!

Write a set of prompts to use for student journaling as part of a unit you have developed in Chapter 3 or 4. Specify the format for your students' journal (handwritten, vlog, podcast, etc.).

Teacher Self-Assessment

Self-assessment and reflection are important not only to students' learning experiences in social justice instruction. Reflection is also key for an educator who prioritizes social justice in the classroom. We encourage you, as an educator, to adopt a **stance of inquiry** toward your planning, teaching and assessment at every stage. A stance of inquiry is a situation in which "practitioners collaboratively theorize, study, and act on those problems in the best interests of the learning and life chances of students and their communities" (Cochran-Smith & Lytle, 2009, p. 123). This approach to thinking critically about teaching and student learning clearly aligns with a social justice orientation.

This section will provide tips for guiding yourself in self-assessment and reflection to best reflect your focus on social justice instruction and help you develop a stance of inquiry toward your work.

Reflective Practice

Reagan & Osborn, in their seminal book *The Foreign Language Educator in Society: Toward a Critical Pedagogy* (2002), suggest that reflective practice empowers teachers to question, "moral, ethical, and other types of normative criteria related directly and indirectly to the classroom" (p. 24). That is, reflective practice can help teachers identify the consequences of their assumptions about their students, class and community, thus helping them make better decisions on how to teach. Reflection is also a type of research, in which you gather information about your students and classroom and then follow a process to report on it. These reports are usually personal but can sometimes be shared with others (Bailey, 2006). Reflection

should occur before, during and after instruction. We will briefly review these three types of reflection, connecting them to questions that can help you reflect on your social justice instruction. Then we will address how this reflection can connect with two frameworks for world language teacher assessment: EdTPA and the TELL Project.

Teacher Reflection at All Stages of Teaching

Reflection *before* instruction, called **reflection-for-practice** (Reagan & Osborn, 2002) or **reflection-on-action** (Bailey, 2006), is often directly connected to lesson planning. Newer teachers might engage more consciously in reflection-for-practice than do more experienced ones. It can include anticipating problems, imagining alternate activities if resources are not available or if time estimates are inaccurate, and thinking through how students might react to instructional practices or materials. When teaching for social justice, reflection before instruction can also address such questions as:

- Are my objectives and activities meaningful and contextualized?

- Do my plans effectively help students achieve the language and social justice objectives I identified at the beginning of my plan?

- Does my classroom reflect equality? That is, do all of my students have equal access to re-sources in the activities I have planned?

- Have I planned and scaffolded a range of activities that prompt my students to use the target language in a variety of ways? Must I pre-teach or create materials to support my students?

- What messages am I sending my students about our priorities in addressing social justice issues by my objectives and lesson structure? Do I want to send them these messages?

- Have I planned for students' differing reactions to this lesson about social justice? What will I do if students do not react in the way I anticipate?

- Have I been inclusive and accurate in how I intend to portray the social justice issues in this lesson, including perspectives from marginalized groups as well as dominant ones? If I am not including some information or some perspectives, why is that?

- Have I provided opportunities or given ideas for the students to take action in response to what they have learned?

Reflection *during* instruction, called **reflection-in-practice** (Reagan & Osborn, 2002) or **reflection-in-action** (Bailey, 2006), concerns your teaching and observation of your classroom's activity so you can fine-tune your instruction as the class continues. This type of reflection is necessarily more rapid than other kinds of reflection; it must happen swiftly so you can react and repair as needed during the instruction process. Issues that reflection during social justice instruction will address include:

- Am I meeting my social justice objectives as expected? If not, am I meeting them in a way that is unexpected?

- What can I do right now to keep us on track and on topic? Do I know where we are heading? Is it where I want to head?

- Does my classroom reflect equity? That is, am I successfully differentiating so I can meet the needs of all students? Are any students struggling? How can I help them?

Reflection *after* instruction, called **reflection-on-practice** (Reagan & Osborn, 2002) or **reflection-on-action** (Bailey, 2006), is perhaps what usually comes to mind when you think about reflective practice. This concerns talking, thinking, writing, or recording your thoughts about the lesson after it has happened. If you find yourself struggling to start, focus on responding to these questions:

- What happened in this lesson? What were important moments in the class that showed how students were (or were not) learning about social justice?

- What was effective or ineffective about the lesson? What evidence do I have for that? (Some areas to consider are: student engagement, student learning, target language use, student understanding of directions or how to do an activity, ratio of teacher-talk to

student-talk, sequence of activities, pacing, use of time, formative assessment, transitions between activities.)

- What am I proud of, especially in terms of how the students learned about social justice? Where was there room for improvement?

- Did I meet the social justice objectives I targeted in the lesson? Why or why not?

- How did the students use the target language as they worked with the social justice content? Is it what I expected and planned? If not, why not?

- What would I change if I were to teach this lesson again?

The format for these forms of reflection is best dictated by your own context and responsibilities as a teacher. Some teachers choose to write a narrative-style reflection on the lesson plan they used, noting the parts of the lesson that were effective and listing changes they would like to make. Other teachers write daily in a notebook dedicated to reflection. Another teacher we knew recorded his reflections with the audio recording feature on his smartphone. Basically, your reflection's format should be the one easiest for you to use and most useful to your future self. If you are a pre-service teacher, you might respond to some of these questions as a part of your coursework and interaction with your cooperating teacher and supervisor. If you are an in-service teacher, you might simply do this as personal professional development, as part of a department or area initiative, or as something that might feed into your formal assessment. In the following sections we will address some of the ways this reflection can connect with your assessment as a teacher, as dictated by two common frameworks for teacher assessment: Teacher Performance Assessment (edTPA) for pre-service teachers (SCALE, 2012), and the *Teacher Effectiveness for Language Learning (TELL) Framework* for in-service teachers (Deering et al., 2011).

Connecting with Frameworks for Teacher Assessment: EdTPA

Teacher Performance Assessment (edTPA), a system of performance-based assessments for novice teachers, has been implemented in many teacher education programs across the U.S. (SCALE, 2017). Based on a portfolio framework and a close examination of 3-5 lessons, teachers using edTPA are guided through specific tasks designed to demonstrate their understanding of teaching and student learning. Importantly, completing the edTPA is one of the few times novice teachers must work independently and cannot seek or receive feedback on anything they create. As such, the more guidance and practice novice teachers can obtain as they approach edTPA, the better.

In this section we will outline reasons why the use of lessons that include social justice instruction can be very helpful to individuals assessed with edTPA. We also provide some brief suggestions for how best to articulate your reflections on social justice instruction in edTPA assessment.

The edTPA World Language Assessment (SCALE, 2017) refers repeatedly to **meaningful cultural contexts.** This term occurs throughout the document in such phrases as "develop communicative proficiency in the target language in meaningful cultural contexts" (2017, p. 1). Since this phrasing prioritizes language over culture, if you choose to use a social justice lesson in your edTPA work, we strongly recommend that you first verify that it is a social justice lesson that focuses on the context of the target culture(s). These cultures need not be defined by national boundaries; they can include the cultures of local communities in which the target language is spoken, including heritage learners and immigrant communities. They can also include points of overlap among your students' cultures and those of speakers of the target language. However, some reflection activities and problem-posing activities could encourage students to examine their own culture(s) exclusively; those types may not be ideal for an edTPA task. We additionally recommend that you clearly articulate your language and social justice objectives, emphasizing how you are using the content to teach specific language concepts and increase students' language proficiency.

In most edTPA items, we would argue that culture is secondary to language objectives. However, one component of *Task 2: Instructing and Engaging Students in Learning* asks, "In what ways will you connect new content

to your students' prior academic learning and personal, cultural, or community assets during your instruction?" (SCALE, 2017, p. 18) Relatedly, "How does the candidate promote comparisons and connections between students' prior experiences and knowledge and the new cultural practices, products, and perspectives of the target language?" (SCALE, 2017, p. 25). The emphasis on students' backgrounds and the lesson's content, particularly cultural content (cultural practices, products, and perspectives), allows inclusion of social justice issues in the lesson. For example, Rubric 8 (SCALE, 2017, p. 25), which focuses on **Subject-Specific Pedagogy,** suggests that this work should be articulated in terms of the lesson's products, practices, and perspectives. As such, you can refer back to Chapter 1, where we describe how social justice activities can reflect the three components of culture in the *World-Readiness Standards for Learning Languages* (NSFLEP, 2014).

Connecting with Frameworks for Teacher Assessment: The TELL Project

The *Teacher Effectiveness for Language Learning (TELL) Framework* (Deering, Duncan, Sauer, & Villareal, 2011) establishes characteristics and behaviors that model world language teachers exhibit. It focuses on teachers' professional growth, so, in addition to clearly defined characteristics and behaviors, the framework also offers feedback and observation tools. The TELL Framework's authors already had issues of access in mind, since they sought to provide access and share resources across all settings in which world language was taught (Alyssa Villareal, personal communication, August 2014). Furthermore, they argued that the TELL Framework enables teachers to reflect on how they "model an attitude of fairness and equity within the context of cross-cultural examination," thus "evidencing behaviors that social justice requires" (Gregory Duncan, personal communication, August 2014).

Note also that many aspects of the TELL Framework strongly connect to the aforementioned ways to create and assess social justice units. Since it is a complex, multi-part framework, in this section we provide a brief overview of how teachers who are assessed or who self-assess using that framework can incorporate it into their social justice instruction.

The TELL Framework is divided into three areas: (1) Preparing for Student Learning, (2) Advancing Student Learning, and (3) Supporting Learning, with seven domains total under these areas. With the help of TELL Framework co-author Gregory Duncan, we have identified the following intersections between the TELL Framework and social justice instruction:

Preparing for Student Learning, in the **Planning** domain, besides echoing the backward design process we have recommended, highlights the importance of:

- guiding students through the examination of products, practices and perspectives (P3.d);

- involving students with a variety of backgrounds and skills (P4);

- engaging them in different levels of thinking, including higher-order thinking (P8.c); and

- considering appropriate authentic materials critically (P9).

By planning social justice instruction as we have described it in this book, you will easily meet these different goals related to **Preparing for Student Learning.**

Under **Advancing Student Learning,** both **The Learning Experience** and **Learning Tools** domains reflect what social justice instruction can bring to your classroom. **The Learning Experience** suggests that the teacher must demonstrate and model respectful classroom behavior (LE1.a), which reflects some of the identity and community issues vital to creating a classroom in which social justice instruction occurs. Additionally, echoing Task 2 in the edTPA model above, the domain criterion of LE6 is a key intersection with social justice: "I provide opportunities for students to engage in cultural observation and analysis." Incorporating social justice objectives into instruction will help you attain a high-level performance on this criterion, which encourages students to recognize and understand aspects of their own culture and others, and to approach a measure of intercultural competence. **Learning Tools** contain numerous references to using tools to access local and global target language communities (LT1.d, LT2.d, LT3.d) and to using authentic materials

and realia (LT1.b, LT3.a, LT3.b); both connect closely to social justice activities that focus on text analysis.

Finally, under **Supporting Student Learning,** the **Collaboration** domain connects your classroom work with local and global communities outside of the classroom (C5), a central component of many of the social justice activities you can undertake with your students. Undertaking rights and policy investigations and individual experience investigations, for instance, would almost certainly give your students new opportunities to learn language. Furthermore, the **Professionalism** domain connects with our original argument that world language teachers model appropriate attitudes and practices with members of other cultures, a vital aspect of teaching for social justice (PR1.a, PR1.b).

Conclusion

Tools for reflection, a key element in teaching world languages through a lens of social justice, provide a powerful space for both teachers and students to reflect on their own experiences, perceptions and roles (Hackman, 2005). On a practical level, reflection and self-assessment can keep you focused on your objectives in teaching social justice lessons. It can help everyone in the classroom understand more about what you are doing and may help you develop as a teacher. However, reflection and self-assessment take time and are not always easy to incorporate into a larger program of instruction and personal development. We encourage you to try one student reflection and one self-reflection activity the first time you implement your social justice unit. If it feels awkward, forced, or time-consuming, find another path to reflection and self-assessment.

Discussion Questions

1. Revisit the vignette about Carol and Oscar. These instructors have student and teacher reflection and self-assessment happening in roughly parallel ways. That is, when the teachers reflect on their work, so do the students. Do you think that this is a good practice? Why or why not?

2. What is the difference between self-assessment and reflection? What do they have in common?

3. Four ways of encouraging student reflection were summarized in the first part of the chapter: self-assessment, peer assessment, portfolios, and journaling. List three positives and three negatives about each of these four paths to student reflection.

4. How can video blogging (vlogging) and podcasting improve on the idea of journaling to encourage student reflection? What are their strengths and weaknesses as alternatives?

5. How do you currently reflect on your work as a teacher (whether a pre-service teacher or an active teacher in the field)? Consider such elements as talking with friends and family, writing email or social media posts, and more formal journaling or reflecting in papers.

6. Both edTPA and the TELL Framework connect with social justice instruction in a number of ways. Can you identify ways, other than those listed, in which you feel your social justice work will satisfy criteria in those models?

REFERENCES

American Council on the Teaching of Foreign Languages. (2017). *NCCSFL-ACTFL Can-do statements.* Retrieved from http://www.actfl.org/publications/guidelines-and-manuals/ncssfl-actfl-can-do-statements

Bailey, K. M. (2006). *Language teacher supervision: A case-based approach.* New York, NY: Cambridge University Press.

Byram, M. (1997). *Teaching and assessing intercultural communicative competence.* Bristol, PA: Multilingual Matters.

Byram, M. (2000). *Assessing intercultural competence in language teaching.* Sprogforum, 18(6), 8-13.

Cochran-Smith, M., & Lytle, S. L. (2009). *Inquiry as stance: Practitioner research for the next generation.* New York, NY: Teachers College Press.

Deering, S., Duncan, G., Sauer, T., & Villarreal, A. (2011). *The teacher effectiveness for language learning (TELL) project.* Retrieved from www.tellproject.org

The National Standards Collaborative Board. (2015). *World-Readiness Standards for Learning Languages.* 4th ed. Alexandria, VA: Author.

Osborn, T. A. (2006). *Teaching world languages for social justice: A sourcebook of principles and practices.* Mahwah, NJ: Lawrence Erlbaum.

Reagan, T. G., & Osborn, T. A. (2002). *The foreign language educator in society: Toward a critical pedagogy.* New York, NY: Lawrence Erlbaum Associates.

Shrum, J., & Glisan, E. W. (2016) *Teacher's handbook: Contextualized language instruction* (5th Ed.) Boston, MA: Heinle.

Stanford Center for Assessment, Learning and Equity (SCALE). (2017). *edTPA World Language Assessment Handbook.* Stanford, CA: Board of Trustees of the Leland Stanford Junior University.

CHAPTER 8
Moving Forward

Throughout the first seven chapters we offered many different ideas and suggestions for teaching social justice in the world language classroom. Now you may still have some lingering questions about how your philosophy of teaching, your context, or your students fit with the notion of teaching for and about social justice. In this section, we will address some of the questions we imagine you might have at this point.

From the teachers we know, we have heard many questions over and over again about the project of teaching languages through the lens of social justice. So we will now address a few burning questions that might remain for teachers seeking to teach for social justice in the world language classroom:

- How can I advocate for teaching for social justice in my classroom? How can I respond to objections from my colleagues, administrators, students and/or parents?

- How can I stay in the target language while teaching for social justice?

- How can I teach for social justice in my elementary world language class?

- How do I recruit and retain students of diverse backgrounds?

- How do I decorate a world language classroom in which social justice is a priority?

- How can I differentiate instruction for all of my learners while teaching for social justice?

How can I advocate for teaching for social justice in my classroom? How can I respond to objections from my colleagues, administrators, students and/ or parents?

Advocacy for teaching for social justice in the world language classroom is sometimes a difficult enterprise. We first suggest you recognize that you need not do this on your own. There are allies you can use for support. Find a trusted colleague who shares your commitment to teaching

for and about social justice—someone with whom you can collaboratively plan and reflect. She or he can also provide emotional support when things go well or not as you had planned. If you do not have a trusted colleague nearby, seek out someone in another geographical area with whom you can establish an online relationship. You can connect with others who share your interest and commitment through professional organizations, including the American Council on the Teaching of Foreign Languages (ACTFL), the National Association for Multicultural Education (NAME), Teachers of English to Speakers of Other Languages (TESOL International), the National Association for Bilingual Education (NABE), and many others.

Fortunately, as world language teachers, many of us are used to advocating for language education. In that vein, we already have an activism-related skillset, so we can readily adapt some of these advocacy actions in an effort to inform other world language educators on teaching for social justice.

Take action by writing letters to textbook companies or the specialist of world language education in your state's education department. Ask them to include content related to social justice issues. Or, more locally, initiate a meeting with your school community's staff and invite them to help you find interdisciplinary connections to some themes you plan to teach. Finally, enlist engaged, creative, or responsive students to share their experiences with others in the school community, including families, administrators, or other school staff. Invite students with particular skills, such as digital video editing or website design, to create products to "show off" to families, the community, and other educators. Ultimately, their voices, particularly when they speak about the knowledge and agency they have gained to improve the world, will be your most influential form of advocacy.

Advocacy largely involves responding effectively to objections as they are expressed to you. As Bell, Washington, Weinstein, & Love (1997) stated, "As we engage with social justice issues and change our classrooms accordingly, we often come into conflict with institutional norms of professed objectivity, authority, and professional distance in ways that can undermine our confidence, lose the support of some of our colleagues, and in some cases jeopardize our positions as faculty" (p. 309). To help individuals who might face objections (or who anticipate doing so), we have summarized some of the main ones below, and some possible responses to them.

Objection A: "More social justice instruction will make it harder to work collaboratively with other teachers." No teacher teaches in a vacuum. If other teachers in a particular context believe languages are important to study and learn for specific reasons, the teacher may feel pressure to conform so she or he can remain in good standing in these relationships. Teachers collaborate with other teachers, following similar scopes and sequences in the curriculum. So you can't just change something without making sure everyone is on board with your intentions.

Response: Start from the assumption that teachers who challenge or criticize the integration of social justice instruction are well-intentioned. Many world language teachers have not had the opportunity to think about how social justice might frame their way of thinking about teaching, or how it might fit into the curriculum. Ask for time to present your units to them so they can see the quality of the work and the learning it encourages. It might also help if you begin slowly with any changes you implement, both for this social reason and for a reason we will explain below—to make the workload manageable. Don't overhaul the entire curriculum right away, or make your colleagues think your previous curriculum was not valuable. If it is your first year teaching, be sensitive to the disruption social justice instruction might represent to your colleagues.

Objection B: "Social justice instruction takes the focus off of language learning." Colleagues who say this might believe that a focus on social justice in the classroom diverts from the "basics," that is, erodes the traditional educational canon. World language teachers in the modern classroom spend a great deal of time trying to engage students with the language, and de-emphasizing language proficiency in favor of other types of issues may not make sense (see also Reagan & Osborn, 2002).

Response: Social justice instruction is best in the world language classroom, when it is fully integrated with language objectives. It offers students ways to use the language in real-life, contextualized ways. Many students are already interested in social justice issues, so presenting them with the options to engage with those topics in their language can be motivating for them for all parts of the class. Again, showing your colleagues your ideas and the outcomes of your students' learning is the best defense here.

Objection C: "The students (and their parents) won't accept this." Teachers teach real students, who might feel confronted by unexpected topics in the classroom. While marginalized students may feel affirmed or empowered by social justice instruction, privileged students might have trouble being asked to reconsider and possibly change their perspective on the world (Swalwell, 2013). Teachers often work with parents (especially at the K-12 level), who might be surprised and challenged by the reports from their children.

Response: Communicate as much as possible about your work with your students and parents (if applicable). You have numerous standards, well-respected literature, and research at your fingertips to demonstrate that an integration of social justice understandings is beneficial for all students in world language classes—share them!

Objection D: "Social justice is about teaching values." Social justice and its focus on societal inequalities can be seen as value-laden or, some might say, political. One might argue that the explicit teaching of values does not belong in the public school classroom, particularly in the U.S., because of the constitutional principle of the separation of government and religion. In the U.S., families are viewed as responsible for teaching values to their children, and some families might have religious or cultural objections to lessons that focus on social justice, particularly in cases where teaching for social justice focuses on certain communities or practices. Furthermore, different teachers or teaching communities might define "social justice" in very different ways, and assuming that it is vital in the same way to all students in all contexts indicates cultural bias (National Council of Teachers of English, 2010). Annam Hasan, an Arabic teacher from Overland Park, Kansas, points out that she is often concerned about skewing her students' perspectives when she teaches topics that contain social justice understandings.

Response: This objection assumes a transmission-of-knowledge model of education, where the teacher imparts information the students must learn and then regurgitate on assessments such as examinations. Social justice education encourages exploration and awareness-building, and students are encouraged to think critically about all perspectives. Yes, this might result in some changing of perspectives, but not as a formal requirement of the instruction. Assessments are not built on students conforming to specific sets of values. Teachers should also recognize that the choice not to take a stance on issues of social justice, or the choice to remain silent, is also a political position.

Objection E: "It is going to take a lot of time and energy to do this." Planning for social justice is reliant on teacher effort and time. Textbooks are often more focused on a U.S. perspective on other cultures, and they rarely broach the subject of social justice issues (Kramsch, 2012; Reagan & Osborn, 2002). As with content-based instruction (CBI), project-based learning (PBL), and other content-oriented types of language instruction, the materials are not available as they are for more communication-based language instruction. To add to this, from a more logistical perspective, many world language teachers must prepare to teach multiple disparate levels, sometimes even traveling between institutions during the workday.

Response: We certainly hope this book will help you with your first line of defense against this objection. We believe it is our responsibility to teach for social justice, and we hope that educators interested in teaching for the success of all of their students will take this responsibility willingly. We know it may cause more work, but our guidelines for creating original units and adapting textbooks will hopefully reduce some of the workload. However, even with these materials, as we stated above, we do recommend starting small. Use prepared materials for some of your curriculum, and add one unit per year or per semester. Give yourself a pilot year for every curricular change. Join or create networks of like-minded colleagues who can support your decision and share resources with you.

How can I stay in the target language while teaching for social justice?

Staying in the target language can be challenging when addressing controversial, emotional, or complex issues, particularly when the class is for novice-level learners. Using the target language consistently in the classroom is one of the Guiding Principles presented by ACTFL (n.d.) for students at all ages and levels of language proficiency. The unit and lesson examples throughout this book provide models for how integration of language and social justice objectives can cover varieties of languages and levels of proficiency. Beyond those models, we have a few suggestions that might help you with integrating social justice education into your classroom.

First, we recommend you use **explicit supports to help students express themselves** in the target language, as you would for any other activity in which the presentational or interpretive modes would be expected. Scaffold the language for students by using sentence frames and teaching them vocabulary and gambits necessary to participate in discussion and other activities. You can keep important vocabulary and gambits posted in your room, or in an online forum throughout a discussion or activity, to give students an easy reference tool. You can also model how to share an opinion or an idea using the vocabulary and gambits.

Similarly, you should **support students in interpreting written and oral texts,** again, as you would for any other interpretive activity. For novice learners, look for texts that are less cognitively demanding or linguistically complex, e.g., image-heavy texts such as infographics that feature numbers and simple phrases; social media posts; captions and illustrations from publications; graphic organizers such as Venn diagrams or mind-mapping; census or statistical information; or texts created for children in the target language. If a desired target language resource is still not at an appropriate language level for your students, you can simplify it yourself by excerpting relevant passages, highlighting important ideas, adding examples, paraphrasing, and/or adding images. If you use a video or a listening activity, you can create a comprehension guide for it that emphasizes its key ideas and focuses students on its vital vocabulary. Technology tools can help you add annotations and pause the video as needed for discussion and clarification.

Another way to stay in the target language in class is to **strategically use English** as a support. Some experts argue that the occasional use of English can be effective in supporting target-language-rich activities and learning (Rosenbusch, 1992). We agree; when the exception to the rule is explicitly explained to the students ("The last ten minutes of class today will be in English"), it can lead to unique learning experiences. The *NCSSFL-ACTFL Intercultural Reflection Tool* (2017) offers the following structure as a framework for reflective activities:

1. an introductory in-class component in the target language;

2. a deeper reflection outside of class in English, or, if the learner's proficiency level allows, in the target language; and

3. a follow-up in-class target language component. (NCSSFL-ACTFL, 2017, p. 1)

As we mentioned in Chapter 6 when discussing critical moments, this structure might sometimes work, particularly for older students with lower proficiency levels. Enabling students to explore complex readings outside of class in English and then processing them together in the target language preserves the target-language-in-class component many teachers seek. However, it also allows for a depth of understanding that supports social justice objectives. Other options for strategically using English might include allowing students to complete reflections in English on simulations carried out in the target language, assessing reading comprehension of target-language texts through English-language questions, and letting students look at translated websites to help them with their understanding of target-language online materials.

Finally, teaching for social justice in the world language classroom has great potential for substantial **connections to content areas** such as social studies, history, environmental studies, and sociology. In this, it may foster collaboration with teachers in other content areas, so your students could learn about some social justice issues both in English (in the content area class) and in the target language (in your class). The students would thereby develop a depth of knowledge from the collaboration involving both classes.

How can I teach for social justice in my elementary world language class?

Research has consistently shown that "children's attitudes toward people different from them appear to develop early and may become more persistent with time" (Rosenbusch, 1992, p. 131). Elementary school teachers at all levels would agree that helping young students to understand how people are the same and different is a key component of their curricula.

This notion of similarity and difference among people is a fundamental concept of social justice education. Stereotypes, misconceptions and untruths based on social and human differences, and the resulting structural inequality and discrimination, are central concepts that social justice education seeks to disrupt and challenge. Though such concepts as discrimination and structural inequality may be harder to address with younger students, a thoughtful presentation of differences among people can lay the groundwork for important social justice instruction as students mature.

For this, we recommend techniques for developing global and multicultural awareness suggested by Curtain & Dahlberg (2016), Rosenbusch (1992) and Picower (2012). Their suggestions include:

- Start with **self-love and knowledge,** where students can discuss and study their own identities and the histories associated with them.

- Help students to focus on **interdependence and relationships** rather than a culture-contrast perspective. That is, allow students to see the variety of countries, regions, and communities, including communities near them, where the language is spoken. Pictures, videos, invited speakers, and Internet resources can support these efforts.

- Acknowledge and build on the cultural differences already present in the classroom by teaching students to **respect others.** Have them identify the ways people differ within their own community and consider those ways from a choice perspective rather than a conflict perspective. Ask the students to perform simple surveys about such subjects as their favorite foods, holidays, and activities, and then link those findings to understandings related to target cultures and issues of social justice.

- Share and explore **events in the target cultures** (historical or current events) that show how people interact and create community. Obvious choices include major international events, such as worldwide celebrations (New Year's Day, harvest festivals) or international sporting events (World Cup, Olympics). Sometimes the international community reacts to events in the U.S., such as a presidential election or a feel-good story, and it is interesting to see their interpretations of such events. Go beyond just exploring the general event and try to help the students imagine what it would be like to be a child of their age experiencing that event.

- Discuss **issues of social injustice** instead of just focusing on celebrating diversity. Elementary students are capable of learning about the history of racism, sexism, classism, homophobia, and other forms of oppression. They can also connect it to current conditions for people today and provide examples they see in their school or community.

- Share histories and examples of **social movement and social change** so that students can understand that cooperation and working together can create change.

- Give students opportunities to **teach others** and **take action on issues.** This can be done through community presentations, letter writing campaigns, grassroots organization campaigns, or attending or organizing protests.

These are good beginnings for teaching for social justice in the elementary world language classroom. Social justice education resources for elementary-age students are becoming more numerous but are still few compared to resources for older students. We recommend the website *Using Their Words* (http://www.usingtheirwords.org/) as a useful tool for teaching young students about social justice and related topics.

How do I recruit and retain students who have ethnicities that are usually underrepresented in language study?

The disparities in world language enrollment among minoritized groups in the U.S. are a significant social justice issue for world language teaching. Although few data report on the racial or ethnic background of students who study languages, we do have student completion data on the Advanced Placement (AP) examination taken by students in upper levels of study. In 2016, of all students who took the AP Exam in one of the seven world language options (Chinese, Spanish, French, German, Italian, Latin, or Japanese), White students (55,102) completed it at a higher rate than other students in most of the seven languages, except for Spanish, in which 104,947 students who self-identified as "Hispanic/Latino" took the exam (The College Board, 2016). The data indicate that only 180 Native American students and 4,516 Black students completed the exam compared to 55,102 White students, meaning that more than ten times as many white students as Black and Native American students combined completed it (The College Board, 2016). A study by Pratt (2012) examined the language enrollment of 7,069 high-school students in an ethnically diverse school district in Texas and found that African-American students' motivation to persist in world language courses and interest in post-secondary study of the language was lower than that of other ethnicities.

A 2007 post-secondary planning survey of college-bound high-school students enrolled in world languages also indicated that African-American students were more likely than students of other ethnicities to opt out of language study after completing their high school requirement, demonstrating a lower rate of persistence (National Research Center for College and University Admissions, 2007).

Therefore, in seeking equity and access in all components of world language education, we must also ensure that all students believe they have a place in the world language classroom. To do this, teachers and schools must first **examine barriers to enrollment in their schools or districts.** Schools can use equity audits (Skrla, McKenzie, & Scheurich, 2009) to examine and interrogate school-based practices, processes, and policies that lead to inequalities in world languages enrollment and achievement. Professional development for faculty and staff can focus on how teachers and counselors may inadvertently discourage underrepresented students from advanced language study through classroom practices, grading practices, and interactions. Steps can be taken to encourage all school stakeholders to consider how world language programs and classrooms can become inclusive spaces for all students to experience growth and success.

Furthermore, you can **envision an inclusive and socially just curriculum** by thinking critically about your implicit biases and the extent to which they inadvertently hold deficit views of students (Battey & Franke, 2015). Today's world language educators must adopt a view that all students can and should learn a language. Around the world, languages and cultures are not limited to just an elite few. People of all different ethnicities, abilities, socioeconomic and religious backgrounds speak a variety of languages and participate in a multitude of cultural practices that reflect their values.

Finally, you can **reach out to minoritized students and families.** World language teachers have significant agency to support practices that can encourage students to begin or continue language study. This can motivate students to pursue initial enrollment in a language study and to persist with it, which can lead to the enrollment of more under-represented students in upper-level language coursework. In the African-American Student Special Interest Group (AAS-SIG) of ACTFL, members have often discussed how they go where the families and students can be found, such as churches, in order to make more personal connections and even offer free lessons to give families an experience with the language and target culture. A two-pronged approach is best: find ways to reach out to students who have not enrolled in a language, but also try to speak with and encourage students who are already enrolled in your language class.

How do I decorate a world language classroom in which social justice is a priority?

As mentioned in Chapter 2, one way to incorporate your students' identities into the classroom is to represent them visually with posters or artwork. One of many methods for this is to find or create visual representations for the walls of the classroom that reflect the diverse identities of your students and the diversity of the target cultures. By providing inclusive visuals in the classroom, you communicate that your world language classroom not only affirms students' identities but also lets them view the target cultures through different lenses. However, it is not always simple to find posters, realia and decorations that represent

a variety of races, ethnicities, abilities, beliefs, and interests. You can search for posters that depict real settings and people, but you may be surprised to find that these posters are often homogeneous in nature. For example, how often are Afro-Latinos or Afro-Germans represented in posters about Spanish-speaking or German-speaking countries? In these cases, there are several ways to find or create more inclusive, diverse visuals.

Art from Target Cultures: Diverse perspectives are celebrated, and social topics are often critiqued, through art in many countries around the world. With some searching you will come across various artists from target cultures that represent different perspectives and reflect some of your students' identities. Use posters, realia, newspapers, images from the Internet, and/or magazine clippings of various artists who depict different races, ethnicities, and abilities and scenes from various segments of society. These images will provide windows into other perspectives and a departure point for discussion. To engage students in more in-depth, critical exploration of art and social justice, lead an artist study over a span of several weeks. Choose one artist from the target culture or an artist from the U.S. who works with target language communities. Make sure the artist's work addresses issues of equity and social justice. Collaborate with your school community's art educators as you choose materials and plan instruction connected to an artist study.

Themed Bulletin Boards: Choose a topic on which you will focus, and create a bulletin board of pictures, articles, realia, art and anything else you can find related to the topic. For example, in a Chinese classroom the bulletin board could represent the theme of environmental justice. Information about pollution in China could be posted, along with rich images from demonstrations led by Chinese citizens calling for action to reduce pollution and create a cleaner environment. The bulletin boards can correspond to topics currently explored in the curriculum or can simply provide a visual way to understand others who are underrepresented in the target cultures.

We, the Students: Involving students in the creation of visuals for the classroom can also be effective. At the beginning of the year, ask students to provide pictures of themselves and attach notecards with their background information written in the target language. With these profiles of your students, you could create a wall collage of all of them so they can see themselves and the diverse backgrounds of other language learners who enter your classroom daily. Your students' visual contributions to the classroom can change throughout the year as you explore and uncover new topics.

In general, be creative and do not limit yourself to commercially made posters. Visuals in your classroom can comprise anything you find. As you travel to countries where the target language is spoken, take care to gather realia that represents different groups of people. Search for articles and pictures on the Internet that provide an underrepresented perspective. The process of decorating the classroom to reflect you, your students, and your objectives is fun as well as important.

Given the benefits of including visual representations of all types of students and members of the target culture, multicultural decorations alone cannot meet the goals of social justice education. Without thoughtful, systematic, well-developed learning opportunities about social justice issues, visual representations may only be "window dressing."

How can I differentiate instruction for all of my learners while teaching for social justice?

Differentiated instruction (Blaz, 2006; Tomlinson, 1999; Tomlinson, 2005), an approach to teaching that recognizes students' similarities and differences, provides scaffolding and challenges for different abilities and lets students to draw from knowledge they have due to their own frames of reference. Differentiation makes it possible for students with a variety of abilities and backgrounds to find success in the world language classroom; though students are working toward common objectives, differentiation provides diverse routes toward those goals. In an equitable classroom, some students need more academic or emotional support while others require more independence. Tomlinson (2005) points out, however, that there is no blueprint for differentiation. While giving teachers the freedom to find an approach that works for their students, she highlights three principles of differentiation that strongly connect with teaching for social justice in world language.

Below we explore these principles and their relationships to Nieto's (2010) components of social justice education, which were highlighted in Chapter 1.

Principle 1: If students have a positive attitude about themselves and about what they are learning, they will experience greater success in the classroom. A primary aim of social justice education is to draw on students' talents and strengths, a recognition all students, regardless of background, appreciate. The teacher thus creates a more positive learning environment and affirms and values students' identities. Furthermore, when students believe the classroom is a place where all abilities and backgrounds are valued, included, and reflected in the learning process, their attitudes about themselves will be more positive and they will find greater success.

Principle 2: Curricula should be designed to engage learners and help the students make meaningful connections between what they are learning and the world. Engagement of students to think critically and meaningfully about their work and look carefully at the world are all components of social justice education as well as differentiated instruction. Although learning vocabulary and grammar are certainly components of the language classroom, learning a world language extends to examining various levels of culture, making comparisons and connections to other disciplines and students' own lives, and extending the language learning process beyond the four walls of the classroom.

Principle 3: Effective differentiation adapts learning and assessments to allow students to reveal their abilities and knowledge. This principle aligns well with the notion that social justice education gives all students the resources necessary to learn to their full potential. Liberating students to take various routes to arrive at common objectives is key in supporting students to reach their full potential. For instance, when a teacher discovered that a high-school German student with a visual processing disability excelled at oral communication and topics related to history, the teacher adapted a written assessment to explain answers orally, thus found out what the student actually knew about the topics learned, and the student was given the resources necessary to succeed (see also Blaz, 2006; Tomlinson, 1999).

Conclusion

The goal of this chapter was to fill in the gaps where questions might linger about ways to integrate social justice instruction into world language classrooms. We hope it has answered any lingering questions you might have and helped you process the very concept of teaching social justice in the world language classroom even further.

Discussion Questions

1. Which of these questions and responses do you feel was most useful to you? Why?

2. What remaining questions do you have? What do you wish we had answered in this chapter?

3. In our response to the question on advocacy, we offered some ideas about why and how you can advocate for social justice instruction. Beyond that section of this chapter, what other parts of this book would help you advocate for social justice in the world language classroom? How would you construct an argument to a skeptical party? Create an advocacy plan.

REFERENCES

American Council on the Teaching of Foreign Languages (ACTFL). (n.d.). *Guiding principles; Use of target language in language learning.* Retrieved from https://www.actfl.org/guiding-principles/use-target-language-language-learning

Battey, D., & Franke, M. (2015). Integrating professional development on mathematics and equity: Countering deficit views of students of color. *Education and Urban Society, 47*(4), 433-462.

Bell, L., Washington, S., Weinstein, G., & Love, B. (1997). Knowing ourselves as instructors. In M. Adams, L. Bell, & P. Griffin (Eds.), *Teaching for diversity and social Justice: A sourcebook.* New York, NY: Routledge.

Blaz, D. (2006). *Differentiated instruction: A guide for foreign language teachers.* New York, NY: Routledge.

Curtain, H. A., & Dahlberg, C. A. (2016). *Languages and learners: Making the match: World language instruction in K-8 classrooms and beyond* (5th Ed.). Boston, MA: Pearson Education.

Kramsch, C. (2012). Editor's introduction to the special issue. *L2 Journal, 4*(1), pp. 1-8.

National Council of State Supervisors for Languages and American Council on the Teaching of Foreign Languages. (2017). *Reflection: Intercultural Communication. NCSSFL-ACTFL Intercultural Reflection Tool.* Retrieved from https://www.actfl.org/sites/default/files/CanDos/Intercultural%20Can-Dos_Reflections%20Scenarios.pdf

National Council of Teachers of English. (2010). *Resolution on social justice in literacy education.* Retrieved from http://www2.ncte.org/statement/socialjustice/

National Research Center for College and University Admissions. (2007). *2007 post-secondary planning survey: Final summary.* Retrieved from https://www.actfl.org/sites/default/files/news/ACTFL_summary_2007_final.pdf

Nieto, S. (2010). *Language, culture, and teaching: Critical perspectives.* New York, NY: Routledge.

Picower, B. (2012). Using their words: Six elements of social justice curriculum design for the elementary classroom. *International Journal of Multicultural Education, 14*(1).

Pratt, C. (2012). Are African-American high-school students less motivated to learn Spanish than other ethnic groups? *Hispania, 95*(1), 116-134.

Reagan, T. G., & Osborn, T. A. (2002). *The foreign language educator in society: Toward a critical pedagogy.* New York, NY: Lawrence Erlbaum.

Rosenbusch, M. H. (1992). Is knowledge of cultural diversity enough? Global education in the elementary school foreign language program. *Foreign Language Annals, 25*(2), 129-136.

Skrla, L., McKenzie, K. B., & Scheurich, J. J. (Eds.). (2009). *Using equity audits to create equitable and excellent schools.* Thousand Oaks, CA: Corwin Press.

Swalwell, K. (2013). *Educating activist allies: Social justice pedagogy with the suburban and urban Elite.* New York, NY: Routledge.

The College Board. (2016). *AP program participation and performance data 2016.* Retrieved from: https://research.collegeboard.org/programs/ap/data/participation/ap-2016

Tomlinson, C. A. (1999). *The differentiated classroom: Responding to the needs of all learners.* Alexandria, VA: Association for Supervision and Curriculum Development.

Tomlinson, C. (2005). Grading and differentiation: Paradox or good practice? *Theory into Practice, 44*(3), 262-269.

APPENDIX A

Selected Social Justice Themes, Activity Ideas, and Online Resources

Disability	
• Students research online policies (government or advocacy websites, building access policy) about individuals with disabilities in different cultures. • Students identify how specific disabilities or classes of disabilities are defined in different cultures. • Students complete graphic organizers to contrast cultures in their work with disabilities, and report on their findings in a paper. • Students identify an inaccuracy or incorrect explanation of a disability on a website in the target language and compose a letter to the organization with correct information. • Students collaborate in groups to write a set of international principles for the treatment of persons with disabilities and then compare it to the *Convention on the Rights of Persons with Disabilities*. • Students use the target language to create a map of their school grounds and the sidewalks leading up to their school from a designated radius. They identify areas accessible for individuals who use wheelchairs or have physical disabilities. They write letters to school administrators about any inaccessible areas and ask for specific changes.	**General information:** http://www.disabled-world.com/disability/awareness/ **International movements related to disabilities:** http://www.un.org/en/events/disabilitiesday/background.shtml
Environment and Climate	
• Looking at published speeches from politicians about the environment in one given country, students examine how different political groups talk about natural resources. They then build off of these speeches to analyze the issue and the different perspectives on it. • Students use sources in the target language to create infographics about issues of environmental justice. They then post them online and publicize them via social media. • Students examine the ways communities of predominantly marginalized groups suffer more from pollution, toxins, and contamination.	**Infographics and articles about climate change:** https://www.connect4climate.org/ **Young people writing about environmental issues:** http://www.voicesofyouth.org/en/sections/environment/pages/environment

Health	
<ul><li>Students identify and discuss their beliefs about access to healthy food by rating how much they agree with such statements as "It's easy to eat healthy food."</li><li>Students, in small groups, define the phrase "food desert" and look at materials in the target language that show where those deserts occur in the target culture(s) or immigrant communities.</li><li>Students create maps to healthy food for communities they study, then share them with the communities via social media or direct contact.</li><li>Students create data tables to display disparate health outcomes among individuals in the U.S. and target cultures along categories of race and ethnicity (e.g., higher rates of premature death from diabetes for African Americans; older Native Americans and Alaska Natives face the highest rates of disability).</li><li>Students label maps from their communities and those in target countries indicating safe areas for affordable housing. They examine these areas in relation to median household income and then create a chart to display their findings.</li><li>Students use authentic readings and videos to understand perspectives on contagious diseases in other cultures. They then create informative posters in the target language to be put up in local hospitals.</li></ul>	**Lesson on food deserts:** http://www.tolerance.org/lesson/food-deserts-causes-consequences-and-solutions **Summaries of a variety of international health concerns:** http://makinghealtheasier.org/ **Young people writing about health:** http://www.voicesofyouth.org/en/sections/health/pages/health **CDC Disparities Analysis:** https://www.cdc.gov/disparitiesanalytics/
Immigration and Refugees	
<ul><li>Students use U.S. Census documents from the government to investigate truths behind immigration in the United States.</li><li>Students watch movies (see *Farmingville* and *Which Way Home*), listen to testimonials (see *Green Card Voices*), or participate in simulations (see *Playing Against All Odds*) that help them to understand issues facing immigrants and refugees in the United States.</li><li>Students connect their experiences and knowledge of immigration to an outreach project in a local immigrant community, based on that community's needs.</li><li>Students hypothesize about the history of immigrants receiving education in the United States: When do they think schools were required to provide support in English? When do they think the segregation of immigrants in schools was outlawed? Then they compare their hypotheses to the real timeline (see PRI source).</li><li>Students use the target language to engage in interviews with volunteers from target cultures in the community to learn about their immigration stories. Then the students create a presentation (written, video, slides, etc.) to document the volunteers' stories.</li></ul>	**US Census information:** www.census.gov **Lesson on immigration myths:** http://www.tolerance.org/sites/default/files/general/tt_immigration_myths.pdf ***Farmingville* movie:** http://www.pbs.org/pov/farmingville/lesson_plan.php ***Which Way Home* movie:** http://whichwayhome.net/ **Timeline of immigration and education:** https://www.pri.org/stories/2015-06-04/brief-history-immigration-and-education-us **Simulation of refugees:** http://www.playagainstallodds.ca/ **Testimonials about being an immigrant in the US:** http://www.greencardvoices.com/

War and Genocide	
<ul><li>Students watch or read about a historical event in the target culture that related to discrimination. Then they work in teams to imagine the different experiences of the actors: the victims, the spectators, the perpetrators.</li><li>Students create poetry and works of art about war and its victims in the target language, modeled on work done by others. Then they display these works around the school or share them in a community art show.</li><li>Students engage in guided exploration using a Webquest activity on the IWitness website through USC's Shoah Foundation (activities and media can be found in eight languages).</li></ul>	**Activities and lessons about discrimination and genocide:** http://iwitness.usc.edu/SFI/Activity/ **Youth writings about war and violence:** http://www.voicesofyouth.org/en/sections/violence–war-and-conflict/pages/violence **IWitness life histories and testimonies of the Holocaust and other genocides:** https://iwitness.usc.edu/sfi/Activity/
Race, Racism, and Discrimination	
<ul><li>Students answer the reflection questions PBS posted on its website about the film *Precious Knowledge*: "Do you think that teaching the history of specific ethnicities promotes a sense among students of their own ethnic superiority? Do you think it's important to dedicate class time to the history of minority groups?" Then they watch the film, return to their original answers, and re-evaluate what they wrote, justifying their responses.</li><li>Students read a story of discrimination based on race in the target language in small groups; each group reads a different story. The teacher can use either authentic stories as they are or simplify the text. The students highlight phrases and words that stand out to them as important and create a word cloud to represent the experience of the person about whom they read.</li><li>Students examine images in media in the target cultures and discuss who is represented and who is missing. They create advertisements that represent those who are missing and share them online through the course website and/or in the school.</li><li>Students play the English-language online game *Killing Me Softly* about microaggressions and conduct a follow-up discussion or written reflection in the target language.</li><li>Students examine implicit racial bias after taking a Project Implicit test. Tests are available in a variety of languages for bias related to age, gender, race, ethnicity, religion, social class, sexuality, disability status, and nationality.</li></ul>	***Precious Knowledge* movie:** http://www.pbs.org/independentlens/films/precious-knowledge/ **Online game "Killing Me Softly" about microaggressions:** http://fobettarh.github.io/Killing-Me-Softly/ **Project Implicit:** https://implicit.harvard.edu/implicit/

Gender	
• Students distinguish between anatomical sex, gender identity, and gender expression using the gender unicorn image in the target language. • Students listen to a read-aloud of a children's picture book that focuses on gender identity in the target language (e.g., *I am Jazz, Morris Micklewhite and the Tangerine Dress; Introducing Teddy*), answer comprehension questions, and/or retell the story of the main character. • Students examine statistics and infographics of gender inequality around the world, comparing and contrasting various countries that speak the target language. They create their own infographic in the target language that depicts these inequalities. • Students explore inequalities in education based on gender in different countries around the world. They summarize their main findings, compare and contrast their findings with their own country, and offer steps that can be taken to improve inequalities in the countries they examined.	**The gender unicorn:** http://www.transstudent.org/gender/ **The Global Gender Gap Report 2016:** http://reports.weforum.org/global-gender-gap-report-2016/ **World Inequality Database on Education:** https://www.education-inequalities.org/

APPENDIX B
Unit Plan Template

Theme and Essential Question(s)

Social Justice Takeaway Understanding(s)

Goals

World-Readiness Standards	Teaching Tolerance Social Justice Standards

Summative Assessments	
Interpretive Communication	
Interpersonal Communication	
Presentational Communication	

Key Formative Assessments/Learning Activities	
Mode of Communication and Objective	Description of Task

APPENDIX C
Sample Unit Plan—All About Me

Theme and Essential Question(s)

All About Me—*What makes up one's identity?*
Target Proficiency: Novice-Mid to Novice-High

Social Justice Takeaway Understanding(s)

Our identities are multifaceted, intersectional, and connected to experiences and membership in different social groups.

Unit Goals

1. Students will be able to describe elements of their identity, including personal characteristics, membership in different social groups, origin, nationality, and age, and compare them with those of others.

2. Students will be able to explain why images from the target culture are stereotypical and do not appropriately describe an individual's identity.

3. Students will be able to define the concept of microaggressions and provide an example in the target language.

World-Readiness Standards	Teaching Tolerance Social Justice Standards
Communication: • Interpersonal, Interpretive, Presentational **Cultures:** • Practices to Perspectives: Cultural practices that are central and important to identity • Products to Perspectives: Characteristics that are central and important to identity **Connections:** • Making Connections: Geography—locations and ethnic backgrounds of speakers of the TL • Acquiring Information and Diverse Perspectives: Reading short bios and watching short videos about people from the target culture in different roles in their communities. **Comparisons:** • Language Comparisons: Adjectives, geographical locations, ethnicities • Cultural Comparisons: Comparing and contrasting students' own identities to bios of people in the target culture they learn about **Communities:** • School and Global Communities: Students learn about each others' identities, sharing and building community with each other in their classroom. • Lifelong Learning: Students will recognize stereotypes for what they are and will be able to look beyond them.	**Identity:** • Students will develop positive social identities based on their membership in multiple groups in society. • Students will develop language and historical and cultural knowledge that affirm and accurately describe their membership in multiple identity groups. **Justice:** • Students will recognize stereotypes and relate to people as individuals rather than representatives of groups.

Summative Assessments	
Interpretive Communication	• Students read three student profiles in the target language that include information about their identities (names, ages, ethnicities, countries of origin, and some things people assume about them). Students complete comprehension questions about the profiles. • Students watch a video about an additional teenager who is an immigrant to the U.S. from a country where the target language is spoken. They fill out a identity card with information about one of the profiles they will use for the interpersonal assessment.
Interpersonal Communication	• Students assume the roles of one of the students and take turns asking and answering questions about their identities. One question must include an incorrect assumption or stereotype about the student the partner must respond to (e.g., "No, I am not Spanish, I am Salvadoran").
Presentational Communication	• Students create a presentational representation of the different facets of their identities. The product is differentiated by student interest, but should include technology (such as slides, a Voicethread, a website, a video, or a PowerPoint presentation) and both spoken and written components. The presentation should include some descriptors they have encountered that others assume about their identities, but that they want to dispel.

Key Formative Assessments/Learning Activities	
Mode of Communication and Objective	Description of Task
Students will be able to describe their physical characteristics and personal qualities. *Presentational Communication*	**Teacher Checklist:** Observation of Total Physical Response (TPR) performance for eight adjectives related to identity markers. **Student Self-Evaluation Checklist Exit Ticket:** How many new words can I identify? How many can I use?
Students will be able to describe their physical characteristics and personal qualities as well as those that others assume about them. *Presentational Communication* *Interpersonal Communication*	**Adapted Circles of My Multicultural Self:** Students complete two versions of the Circles Activity (see Chapter 2): one based on what others assume about them, the other based on their actual identity elements. **Assumptions or truths:** Students use the circles activity to ask each other about elements of their identities, providing yes/no answers about the assumptions and truths.
Students will be able to describe their physical characteristics and personal qualities, noting the areas where there are intersections. *Presentational Communication* *Interpersonal Communication*	**Peer Characteristics Scavenger Hunt:** Students walk around and write names of classmates on a worksheet who fit the identity markers on the worksheet. **"I am..." Presentational Writing:** Students write short statements and include collage/visual representations, emphasizing areas of intersection.
Students will be able to tell their ages and ask a friend his/her age. *Interpersonal Communication*	**Teacher Checklist:** Could they do it? 30-second partner performance-based assessment.

Students will be able to compare and contrast their ages and physical characteristics with others. Students define microaggressions and provide examples in the target language. *Interpretive Communication* *Presentational Communication*	**Characteristics Venn Diagram:** Students read one of their classmates' "I am" descriptions from Day 2 and compare their characteristics with those of two classmates. **Microaggression Examples Poster:** After watching a short video about microaggressions, students brainstorm some microaggressions in the target language. In their L1, they explain why these microaggressions are hurtful, insensitive, or stereotypical. The poster becomes the basis for a hallway display to teach other students about microaggressions.
Students will be able to tell someone where they are from. *Interpretive Communication* *Presentational Communication*	**Social Justice (SJ) Heroes:** Posters depicting the name, country of origin and characteristics of various social justice leaders will be hung around the room. Students walk around and write a statement about where they are from. **Tech-Oral Exit Ticket:** Students tweet or Instagram a picture and statement about where they are from and then say the statement on the way out.
Students will be able to tell someone their age and where they are from. *Interpersonal Communication*	**Teacher Checklist:** Could they do it? 15-second individual performance assessment.
Students will be able to compare their geographical origins with those of others. *Interpretive Communication* *Presentational Communication*	**Homework Comparison Table:** Create a comparison chart of origins based on the results of the in-class interpersonal communicative activity and social justice poster activity from earlier in the unit. Then calculate class wide percentages of individuals representing different ethnicities, ages, and additional identity markers.
Students will be able to compare their geographical origins with those of others. *Presentational Communication*	**All About Me Technology-based Project:** Students use various forms of technology (differentiated as appropriate) to create an "all about me" illustration. This is assessed with a mini-project rubric.
Students will be able to analyze the stereotypes inherent in images of people from the target culture. *Interpretive Communication*	**Before and After Survey and Reflection:** Students complete a Perceptions and Stereotypes survey (in their L1) before and after the lesson. Then they analyze their own growth that occurred between the surveys.
Students will be able to explain why images from the target culture do not appropriately describe an individual's identity. *Presentational Communication*	**Image Description:** In groups, students write and then present 3-4 statements describing the individual's or image's characteristics (in TL). **Problem-posing Analysis and Reflection:** Students analyze the possible stereotypes in their images. They present this in their L1 on a poster. With a poster carousel, groups add to posters with additional thoughts.

APPENDIX D

Lesson Plan Template

Lesson Plan Template from *Keys to Planning for Learning: Effective Curriculum, Unit, and Lesson Design* by Clementi & Terrill (2017)

Language Level		Grade		Date		Day in Unit		Minutes	
Unit Theme and Question									
Daily topic:									

STANDARDS		LESSON OBJECTIVES		
What are the communicative and cultural objectives for the lesson?	Communication and Cultures	Which modes of communication will be addressed?	Students can:	
		☐ Interpersonal		
		☐ Interpretive		
		☐ Presentational		
If applicable, indicate how Connections, Comparisons, Communities, and Common Core will be part of your lesson.	Connections			
	Comparisons			
	Communities			
	Common Core			

Lesson Sequence	Activity/Activities What will learners do? What does the teacher do?	Time* How many minutes will this segment take?	Materials, Resources, Technology Be specific. What materials will you develop? What materials will you bring in from other sources?
Gain Attention/ Activate Prior Knowledge			
Provide Input			
Elicit Performance/ Provide Feedback			
Provide Input	*If applicable*		
Elicit Performance/ Provide Feedback	*If applicable*		
Closure			
Enhance Retention & Transfer			
Reflection – Notes to Self • What worked well? Why? • What didn't work? Why? • What changes would you make if you taught this lesson again?			

For additional details, see Clementi, D., & Terrill, L. (2017). *The keys to planning for learning: Effective curriculum, unit, and lesson design.* Alexandria, VA: ACTFL.

APPENDIX E

Sample Unit Plan Overviews

Elementary All Languages: Novice-Mid to Novice-High

Theme/Social Justice Issue: Wants versus Needs

Essential Question: How do I define what I want versus what I need?

Social Justice Takeaway Understandings:

- There are many ways to be rich.
- Advertisement and commercials can influence how I feel about what I do and do not have.

Language Objectives:

- Students will be able to describe their possessions by using positive and negative expressions such as "I have," "I do not have," "I need," "I do not need" with appropriate vocabulary to describe material possessions as well as non-material riches.

- Students will be able to use words to describe their emotions: jealous, unhappy, happy, proud.

- Students will be able to identify and define new vocabulary words that correspond with material and non-material possessions.

Activities:

1. As a class, students brainstorm a list of things children might generally have, but make those children who don't have them feel jealous, e.g., specific articles of clothing or technology. Students choose five new words to keep track of in their notebook. For each word, they draw a picture or write about a memory they think will really help them recall this word.

2. Students write a sentence in the target language and draw a picture illustrating an experience they can remember of having something someone else wanted. Then they write a sentence in the target language and draw a picture illustrating an experience they can remember of someone else having something they wanted. In a group, they talk about these experiences. Then, in a group or as a class, they list words describing their emotions about having and not having certain things.

3. Students examine common magazine ads and/or pictures from the target culture or their own culture. They identify how those ads make them feel about the possession.

4. As a class, students brainstorm a list of non-material possessions they can have.

5. In small groups, students create magazine ads or commercial skits advertising a non-material possession that can make them rich. They share their ads or skits with the class, and compare them to the pieces of media you critiqued as part of the lesson.

Adapted from the Teaching Tolerance website: https://www.tolerance.org/classroom-resources/tolerance-lessons/wants-versus-needs-0

Elementary All Languages: Novice-Mid to Novice-High

Theme/Social Justice Issue: Improving our Community

Essential Question: How can I contribute positively to my community?

Social Justice Takeaway Understandings:

- I am responsible for my community.
- I can make changes in my community when I speak up.
- Kids everywhere can make changes in their community.

Language Objectives:

- Students will be able to discuss and defend their preferences by using such phrases as "I prefer [...] because..." and "I don't like [...] because..."

- Students will be able to ask for more information by formulating questions using such question words as "Why" and "How."

- Students will be able to use and recognize vocabulary related to caring for the school environment in order to understand the example service projects and create one of their own.

Activities:

1. Students see examples of three service projects being done in the target language-speaking elementary schools in the target language-speaking city.

2. Students make a pamphlet in the target language about how to be peaceful in school and avoid conflicts with other students.

3. Students create fake tickets they can give people in the school whom they see acting nicely or paying attention to the environment.

4. Students watch a few student-made videos in the target language that give instructions on how to save energy and recycle responsibly.

5. Students choose their service project by voting.

6. Students contact the schools that did the projects and see if they have any advice to help them. They prepare a set of questions ahead of time to find out about the other students.

7. Students carry out their service projects.

Unit Adapted from a Project at Ecole François-de-Laval, Montréal

Secondary Chinese: Novice-High to Intermediate-Low

Theme/Social Justice Issue: Resources and Opportunities

Essential Question: How does my privilege affect resources and opportunities I may have?

Social Justice Takeaway Understandings:
- We should think about limitations in resources and opportunities for different groups of people.
- We should recognize our own privilege and the effects it has on our lives.

Language Objectives:
- Students will be able to compare the differences between the opportunities they have and those other groups of people in China have, specifically focusing on "migrant families" in China.
- Students will be able to list different opportunities they have living in the U.S.
- Students will be able to describe the quality of primary necessities, using vocabulary such as good education, healthy foods, clean showers, new clothing, etc.

Activities:

1. In groups, students brainstorm the opportunities they have as teenagers in the U.S. Then they research different opportunities other teenagers in the U.S. have and don't have. After students realize the differences in opportunities in their country, the teacher can introduce the students to the lifestyles of children their age in China through visuals (videos and images).

2. Students watch a movie or part of a movie that depicts the living conditions of children in rural China. The students can then reflect on the different opportunities the children have or don't have by filling out a graphic organizer and writing about what they learned.

3. Jigsaw Discussion: Prepare 2-4 separate materials (readings and/or images) on people in China. Ask each student to investigate one of the materials individually and answer comprehension questions. Then, group the students into their "expert groups" (with others who investigated the same material) and ask them to ask each other clarifying questions and compare answers to make sure they know their material well. Finally, arrange the students into groups with those who investigated different materials to teach each other what they learned. Make sure the students are taking notes on what they are learning from their peers. As a follow-up, ask each student to write a paragraph about she or he learned from all of the materials.

4. As a class, students categorize different resources into groups such as sanitation, clothing, education, foods, etc. Assign groups of students to each category and ask them to do further research on them. Then ask the students to prepare presentations comparing the resources and opportunities of teenagers in the U.S. to those in China under their assigned categories.

Unit overview written by Ngan-Ha Ta

Secondary French: Novice-Mid to Novice-High

Theme/Social Justice Issue: Stereotypes of the French Culture

Essential Question: How can stereotypes affect my understanding of the French culture?

Social Justice Takeaway Understandings:

- We have many common stereotypes of other cultures, and these stereotypes are created and maintained in a variety of ways.
- Preconceived notions of other cultures impact the way human beings live and experience the world they inhabit.

Language Objectives:

- Students will be able to engage in a variety of reading, writing and speaking activities with consistency in both past and present tenses.
- Students will be able to organize and categorize stereotypes.
- Students will be able to identify commonly stereotypical things in the target culture and report on identification of the stereotypes of the target culture in U.S. media with such verbs as "to see," "to find," "to discover," and "to read."

Activities:

1. Students draw, write, or find examples of what they think are typical things in the target culture, using terms they brainstorm as directed by the teacher.

2. They will look at examples of stereotypes of the U.S., using websites and books about the U.S., thus examining stereotypes and their relationship with the truth. They will categorize them according to the categories of cultural myths, generalizations, or cultural realities, and if they are positive or negative. They will discuss possible origins of the stereotypes.

3. The teacher will show movies, books, pictures, and websites that reflect the same stereotypes of the French culture the students generated in Activity 1. Students can also be assigned to find their own examples and present them to the class.

4. Students will then examine the truth behind the stereotypes of the French culture, researching them through articles and videos and then categorizing them as cultural myths, generalizations, or cultural realities. They will then create posters and presentations to share within and beyond the classroom to educate others about the truth behind stereotypes of the French culture.

Original unit written by Pam Wesely about French stereotypes: http://carla.umn.edu/cobaltt/lessonplans/frames.php?unit-ID=90

Secondary or Post-Secondary Japanese: Intermediate-Low to Intermediate-Mid

Theme/Social Justice Issue: Foreign Labor in Japan Today

Essential Question: What is it like to be a foreign worker in Japan? How are Japanese residents and the Japanese government reacting to a changing workforce demographic?

Social Justice Takeaway Understandings:
- People choose to immigrate to many places for many reasons.
- Countries have a responsibility to their laborers regardless of the nationality, education level or status of those laborers.

Language Objectives:
- Students will be able to compare points of view using the structure 〜にとって.
- Students will be able to describe positive and negative aspects of life in Japan for foreign laborers and their employers using 〜やすい and 〜にくい.
- Students will be able to analyze a job posting for important details.

Activities:
1. Students compare points of view within the context of local restaurants and their employees.
   a. Students identify a local restaurant and explain their choices in small groups.
   b. Students explain why they like (or dislike) the restaurant, contrasting personal points of view (food preferences, allergies, locations, etc.).
   c. Digging deeper, students reflect on what it might be like to work there based on the information they have (short hours vs. working a grill; no table service vs. a lot of cleaning at a buffet, etc.).

2. Students read Japanese job descriptions, choosing one they find interesting.
   a. Students build work-related vocabulary by analyzing job postings in pairs and by brainstorming additional terms for job-seekers.

3. Students watch a video on foreign workers in the Gunma Prefecture.
   a. Before watching the video, students brainstorm positive and negative aspects of a large foreign workforce from the perspective of a Japanese resident of Gunma.
   b. After watching the video, students compare notes to identify the opinion of the report on foreign residents and to discuss any bias they might detect.

4. Students consider the other side: They will read English-language articles on refugee workers and government response to urgent workforce needs outside of class to provide additional information and will summarize the content of the article in class in Japanese.

References

BBC World Service. (2017, May 1). *Japan's exploited foreign workers* [BBC Podcast, 17:48]. Retrieved from https://www.bbc.co.uk/programmes/p050y2sv

Indeed [Japanese]. (n.d.) Retrieved from http://jp.indeed.com

Infographic on declining workforce & strategies. (n.d.). Retrieved from https://info-graphic.me/wp-content/uploads/2014/10/037b398e209ed35b08f914f5900c723b.png

Kikuchi, D., & Tanaka, C. (2018, January 12). Japan toughens screening rules for refugees; automatic work permits ditched. *The Japan Times*. Retrieved from https://www.japantimes.co.jp/news/2018/01/12/national/japan-tighten-refugee-screening-system-starting-next-week/#.WyrMgvQrLrd

NHK. (2016, October 11). シリーズ あなたの働き方が変わる!? コンビニで急増!?留学生バイト 〜外国人労働者100万人時代へ〜 *NHK News Web*. Retrieved from http://www.nhk.or.jp/gendai/articles/3873/1.html

NHK. (2016). 関東地方の在留外国人（2016年12月）*Japan Broadcasting Corporation*. Retrieved from http://www.nhk.or.jp/syakai/10min_tiri/shiryou/pdf/017/shiryou_001.pdf

NHK. (2018, October 15). 求む！外国人正社員 *NHK News Web*. Retrieved from https://www3.nhk.or.jp/news/html/20180517/k10011440501000.html?utm_int=detail_contents_news-related_002

NHK. (2018). なぜ群馬県には多くの外国人が暮らしているの？[VIDEO]. *NHK for School*. Retrieved from http://www.nhk.or.jp/syakai/10min_tiri/?das_id=D0005120467_00000

Osumi, M. (2018, January 2). Abuses still abound in labor-strapped Japan's foreign 'trainee' worker system. *The Japan Times*. Retrieved from https://www.japantimes.co.jp/news/2018/01/02/national/abuses-still-abound-labor-strapped-japans-foreign-trainee-worker-system/#.WzYdq6dKjrc

Yoshida, R. (2017, December 31). Japan's need for foreign labor to get dire as 2050 nears. *The Japan Times*. Retrieved from https://www.japantimes.co.jp/news/2017/12/31/national/japans-need-foreign-labor-get-dire-2050-nears/#.WyrUAqdKjre

ローソンの外国人社員採用 について (n.d.). [Company Paper]. Retrieved from http://www.kantei.go.jp/jp/singi/jinzai/jitsumu/dai3/siryou2_3.pdf

Unit overview written by Sara Biondi

Secondary Latin: Novice-Mid to Novice-High

Theme/Social Justice Issue: Slavery in the Ancient World

Essential Questions:

- How did the ancient Roman economy function?
- How do modern readers know about the lives of ancient people?
- What did the Romans believe about non-Romans?

Social Justice Takeaway Understandings:

- The ancient world was built through unpaid labor.
- The texts that survived into the modern age are missing the voices of the oppressed.
- Beliefs about the humanity of individuals impacted Roman slavery and citizenship.

Language Objectives:

- Students will be able to comprehend texts about slavery and interpret the meaning behind use of the imperfect and perfect tense.
- Students will be able to comprehend texts about slavery by applying vocabulary related to enslaved peoples.

Activities:

1. Students will retell stories from the non-Roman character's point of view.

2. Students will view authentic artifacts and discuss their use, applying the See-Think-Wonder thinking routine (from Project Zero).

3. Students will read *Frederick Douglass: The Last Day of Slavery* and contrast it with the ancient Roman practices of slavery.

4. Students will read Horace's *Odes* 1.38 and explain the role of the enslaved *puer*.

5. Students will be able to explain the ways class status affected the lives of Roman citizens.

6. Students will be able to explain the impacts of colonization and Roman slavery.

7. Students will engage in problem-posing activities, text analysis, artifact analysis, rights and policy investigations, and reflection activities.

Unit overview written by Elissabeth Legendre and Whitney Hellenbrand

Secondary Latin: Novice-High to Intermediate-Low

Social Justice Issue/Topic: Gender; Daphne & Apollo, Ovid, *Metamorphoses*, I.452-567

Essential Questions:

- How did gender determine destiny in the ancient world?
- How does Ovid's *Metamorphoses* reflect the era in which it was written?

Social Justice Takeaway Understandings:

- Romans believed that the role of women was to marry a husband chosen for her by her father.
- Roman believed that a woman's purpose was to bear her husband's offspring.
- Romans believed that a woman's virginity was so valuable it was better to be dead than violated.
- Many parts of the *Metamorphoses* can be read as pro-Augustus propaganda.

Language Objectives:

- Students will be able to explain traditional Roman gender roles and values.
- Students will be able to discuss how Roman gender roles and values limit choices for Romans.
- Students will be able to recognize and describe examples of pro-Augustus propaganda.
- Students will be able to compare and contrast ancient and modern beliefs about sexuality.
- Students will be able to comprehend poetry in dactylic hexameter.
- Students will be able to understand unadapted authentic texts from the Augustan period.

Activities:

1. Students will read and summarize Ovid's Daphne and Apollo (*Metamorphoses* I. 452-567).

2. Students will perform a See-Think-Wonder routine for Bernini's Apollo and Daphne statue.

3. Students will discuss how rhetorical devices reinforce Daphne's helplessness.

4. Students will analyze ancient and modern roles of choice and who controls a woman's body.

5. Students will read about Augustan marriage laws and discuss their effects on Daphne and Apollo.

6. Students will compare and contrast propaganda and fake news.

7. Students will engage in problem-posing activities, text analysis, artifact analysis, rights and policy investigations, and reflection activities.

Unit overview written by Elissabeth Legendre and Whitney Hellenbrand

Secondary Russian for Heritage Learners: Novice-High to Intermediate-Low

(Original Unit from Concordia Language Villages for Credit Villagers)

Theme/Social Justice Issue: Standards of Beauty in Russian Art, Poetry, and Film

Essential Questions: How is beauty defined and created in Russian paintings, poetry, and films throughout history? How can beauty be defined in different ways?

Social Justice Takeaway Understandings:
- Standards of beauty do not define one's self worth.
- There is value in everyone and in many forms of beauty.

Language Objectives:
- Students will be able to describe standards of beauty throughout Russian history.
- Students will be able to identify images of beauty in Russian poems and films.
- Students will be able to compare and contrast Russian standards of beauty with beauty standards around the world and within their own culture.
- Students will be able to describe how standards of beauty reflect norms of culture and society.
- Students will be able to persuade others that beauty can be found in many forms.

Activities:

1. Students read and watch a variety of history Russian text (poetry, advertisements, film)

2. Students describe standards of Russian beauty throughout history and justify their descriptions based on evidence in the text.

3. Students hypothesize standards of beauty in Russia today.

4. Students examine modern advertisements, commercials and other authentic texts, comparing and contrasting modern beauty standards with historical ones. Who is represented? How is beauty defined? How is the definition of Russian beauty incomplete?

5. Students complete a WebQuest to compare and contrast Russian standards of beauty with beauty standards from around the world and within their own culture.

6. Students work in small groups to create a short presentation about how they believe standards of beauty reflect norms of culture in Russia compared to two other cultures, providing evidence to justify their beliefs.

7. Students use an authentic text they read previously and rewrite a poem or recreate an advertisement to demonstrate inclusivity of all definitions of beauty within Russian culture.

8. Students create a PSA to persuade others to expand their definitions of beauty.

Unit overview written by Leyla Masmaliyeva, Lara Ravitch, and Becky Blankenship

Secondary Spanish: Novice-High to Intermediate-Low

Theme/Social Justice Issue and Topic: Childhood; Child Labor and Mate

Essential Questions: Why does child labor exist? How does child labor relate to cultural products of importance such as mate production? Is fair trade "fair?"

Social Justice Takeaway Understandings:
- Children's daily lives may be punctuated by various challenges.
- Child labor takes place in many countries, including Argentina, to produce products important to the culture.
- As consumers, we must know where products come from and how they are produced.

Language Objectives:
- Students will be able to describe cultural products and practices they see in images and read in texts.
- Student will be able to ask questions about mate production.
- Students will be able to explain their opinions about tea, mate production, and unfair labor practices using details and examples.
- Students will be able to explain why child labor exists and its consequences.

Activities:

1. Students view images of posters that protest child labor in Argentina. Students examine the images, note new vocabulary, and gather ideas about arguments against child labor.

2. Students read an article about child labor in Argentina and list its causes and consequences.

3. Students will write a letter to the head(s) of one of the mate producers in Argentina expressing their concerns about child labor practices by comparing the experiences of those children with their own childhood and offering suggestions for what can be done to remedy the situation and improve the quality of life for the families involved in mate harvesting and production.

4. After completing the final draft of the letter, students will create a visual component to complement and emphasize their message. This could take the form of a poster modeled after the images they previewed, or any other visual message of their choosing. The visual aid could be digital, interactive, or two- or three-dimensional, or students could propose another medium of their choice. Depending on the medium, these images could either accompany the letter or be posted in the school or community to draw additional awareness to the issue of child labor practices worldwide.

Unit overview written by Alyssa Warne

Secondary or Post-Secondary Spanish: Novice-Mid to Novice High

Theme/Social Justice Issue: Pastimes and Sports; Equity and Access in Sports and Activities

Essential Question: How is access to and experience with pastimes and sports influenced by socioeconomic status, ability, culture, and technology?

Social Justice Takeaway Understandings:

- The type of pastimes and sports we practice are influenced by our economic status, abilities and cultural background.
- The way in which sports and other activities are adapted for people with disabilities varies from one culture to the next.
- Due to strong cultural traditions, some pastimes still remain unchanged.
- Technology is modifying pastimes activities in urban areas.

Language Objectives:

- Students will be able to describe their favorite pastimes and reflect on the reasons why they like those activities.
- Students will be able to identify the most popular sports in their country and compare them to most popular sport practiced in Spanish speaking countries.
- Students will be able to summarize the role technology plays in their free-time activities.

Activities:

1. Students do the Google search *"Deportes más populares en Estados Unidos"* in images to reflect on how these media portray the most popular sports in the U.S. Students express their agreement or disagreement with the information and statistics they find, and then they do a survey by interviewing a group of classmates to identify the most popular sports in the class and find reason why they like them.

2. Students watch a video in the target language of a group of five-year-old children playing soccer in a dirt open field and are asked to describe what they see in the video. They receive guiding questions inquiring about the ages of the kids, the excitement the kids have for playing soccer, and the equipment they need to play it. Students reflect on the differences between sports that do not require much equipment like soccer with sports that do require expensive equipment like hockey. They see how their economic status determines the sports they play.

3. Students read a simple biography of a famous soccer player who was born and grew up in a low-income family and neighborhood. They follow questions on a comprehension guide to assist them with their understanding, and they present their reactions to the reading. Students compare the soccer player biography to the biography of a famous American player to analyze the challenges these people faced in their early careers.

4. Students complete a WebQuest about Spanish-speaking athletes who have competed in the Paralympics and examine hurdles they have had to overcome to train for their sport in an adaptive manner. What kind of support exists for athletes with disabilities in their cultures? Where and how do they train?

5. Students discuss other pastime activities they like, besides sports, to reflect on the role technology plays in their daily life and in their leisure time. They work in pairs to search the web to present on the positive and negative effects of the influence of technology in the free time activities of young people in the US and one Spanish speaking country.

Unit overview written by Fanny Roncal Ramirez

Post-Secondary Arabic: Intermediate-Low to Intermediate-High

Social Justice Issue/Topic: Diversity and Inclusivity; The Syrian Refugee Crisis

Essential Questions: What does it mean to be a refugee? How can refugees' new country help them to resettle and feel welcome?

Social Justice Takeaway Understandings:

- There are different reasons that force Syrians to leave their homes.
- Syrian Refugees face many difficulties when they have to settle in a new country.
- We have many responsibilities towards the refugees and we have to explore ways to help them.

Language Objectives:

- Students will be able to describe what a refugee is.

- Student will be able to describe the Syrian refugee crisis and the historical context that led them to this current situation.

- Students will be able to analyze arguments for and against helping refugees and evaluate our duty to protect other people's human rights.

Activities:

1. Show pictures of refugees to the students and ask the students to guess what that word might mean based on the pictures.

   a. Ask the students to work in pairs, and provide them with a definition of a refugee in the target language.

   b. Ask the students about the different reasons people are forced to leave their homes and discuss how they would feel if they were a refugee.

2. Introduce students to the Syrian refugee crisis and its historical context by showing them a video displaying the story of how a Syrian family fled from Syria to resettle in a new country. Let the video serve as a stimulus for the students' creation of a thoughtful performance about leaving home.

3. Students do a role-play in which they imagine that they are forced to leave the country and discuss who should go first and what that person should take along.

   a. The teacher assumes the role of an Immigration Officer at passport control. The students who were agreed upon to leave the country will be investigated at border control. They will need to convince the officer of their story so they can be allowed into the new country as refugees.

   b. After the role-play, the teacher will discuss with the class their reactions to the experience of being an asylum seeker, and whether it has changed their perception of refugees in this country?

4. Students will research organizations that work with refugees. From their findings, the students will prepare an interactive poster that will be used to share key steps the organization takes to support refugees. Students will share their posters with each other in a gallery walk, writing notes about each organization to be used for small-group and whole-class discussion after the gallery walk.

Unit overview written by Asma Ben Romdhane

Post-Secondary Spanish: Intermediate-Low to Intermediate-High

Theme/Social Justice Issue: Hispanic Immigration; Child Immigration

Essential Questions:

- Why and how do children migrate?

- What kinds of complex issues are involved in child migration? What kind of role can I play in supporting migrant children and their families?

Social Justice Takeaway Understandings:

- Migration has been a human endeavor all over the world in all times.

- Violence and various political and economic conditions force families to leave their countries.

- Children migrate with their families or by themselves because their parents are very concerned about their safety in their hometowns or home countries.

Language Objectives:

- Students will be able to express opinions on topics related to Hispanic immigration to the U.S., express possibilities for immigrants, and make suggestions on proper treatment of immigrants.

- Students will be able to identify the main reasons why families leave their home countries and migrate to the U.S.

- Students will be able to debate their stance on the topic of child immigration to the U.S.

Activities:

1. Students watch the film *La Misma Luna* to identify the reasons why the main character, a nine-year-old boy, leaves his town and decides to come to the U.S. all by himself. Students talk about what they would do if they were in the same situation.

2. Students read the text *La Travesía: Migración e Infancia* by UNICEF to learn about child migration from an international perspective. They follow questions on a comprehension guide to assist them with their understanding and to focus their attention to the data related to child migration to the U.S., its causes, and its consequences for the child.

3. In pairs, students receive the biography of a child from either Mexico or a Central American nation. The biography includes information about the child's specific place of origin, family background and economic status, as well as the political situation of the child's home country. After reading the biography, students will give presentations on where they believe the child would have a better future.

4. Students write a letter to the President of the United States expressing their stances on the topic of child migration using factual arguments.

Unit overview written by Fanny Roncal Ramirez

Assessment Rubrics

Rubric 1: Sample Holistic Social Justice Rubric to be added to an Integrated Performance Assessment (IPA)
Building off of the IPA rubric created by Glisan, Adair-Hauck, Koda, Sandrock, & Swender (2003; see also Sandrock, 2015), we suggest that a social justice component be added to an IPA rubric for a social justice lesson. This will vary greatly according to the IPA, but this is a general example.

	Exceeds Expectations	Meets Expectations	Does Not Meet Expectations
Social Justice Understanding To what extent can the student identify or explain the intended understanding?	Demonstrates a complex, detailed understanding of the social justice issue.	Demonstrates appropriate understanding of the social justice issue.	Demonstrates limited understanding of the social justice issue.
Content Knowledge Does the student show sufficient mastery of the major non-linguistic concepts, data, and/or other factual information in this unit?	Provides a clear, accurate representation of the content information and arrives at insightful conclusions.	Provides an accurate representation of the content information with sufficient mastery.	Provides inaccurate representation of content information by leaving out critical details.
Critical Thinking Does the student's work show an appropriate level of critical thinking and perspective-taking?	Approaches the social justice issue thoughtfully and critically, taking into account a variety of perspectives.	Approaches the social justice issue thoughtfully and critically.	Approaches the social justice issue with no evidence of critical thinking or thoughtfulness.

Rubric 2: Can-Do Statements for Social Justice Instruction

Can-Do Statements, like the *NCSSFL-ACTFL Can-Do Statements* (ACTFL, 2017), can offer students an opportunity to reflect on their own practice. This rubric offers some general suggestions at the different levels outlined by Sandrock (2010). Much of this has also been adapted from LinguaFolio Wisconsin: Culture (from www.waflt.org).

Level: Beginning	I can do this somewhat.	I can do this well.	This is my goal.
I can identify the important parts/actors in this social justice issue.			
I can repeat the arguments on each side of this debate.			
Level: Developing	I can do this somewhat.	I can do this well.	This is my goal.
I can explain the main points of a social justice issue accurately using simple sentences.			
I can explain the impact of one aspect of a social justice issue on daily life.			
Level: Transitioning	I can do this somewhat.	I can do this well.	This is my goal.
I can compare and contrast different perspectives relating to a social justice issue accurately.			
I can explain the impact of one aspect of a social justice issue on people's beliefs, perspectives, and attitudes.			
Level: Refining	I can do this somewhat.	I can do this well.	This is my goal.
I can critique, examine, and weigh the multiple perspectives and components of a social justice issue.			
I can explain the impact of the social justice issue on a variety of things, including politics, economics, history, etc.			

Index